Railtracks in the Sky

'New' Labour,
Air Transport Deregulation
and the Competitive Market

By
Peter Reed

SPOKESMAN
for
SOCIALIST RENEWAL

First published in 2002 by
Spokesman
Russell House, Bulwell Lane
Nottingham
NG6 0BT
Phone 0115 9708318.   Fax 0115 9420433. ·
e-mail elfeuro@compuserve.com
www.spokesmanbooks.com

ISBN 0 85124 671 0

A CIP Catalogue is available from the British Library.

Printed by the Russell Press Ltd (phone 0115 9784505).

Contents

Preface

I have to thank Ken Coates and Mike Hogarth for suggesting this work. I was at first reluctant to take it on because it is hard to do justice to such a complex subject in any reasonable brevity. Indeed, as I look back over the text, I see many places where I would like to provide more background, add extra detail and perhaps insert some qualifications. I can only hope that the notes and references will help to counter any risk of over compression.

I am not an academic and write mainly from personal experience. Originally, I therefore intended to keep references to a bare minimum. But in view of the huge gap between the reality and the picture of it set out in official documents and academic texts, I felt it necessary to quote authorities for many statements. In some cases, the official doctrines are so silly that, without detailed sources, people might believe I was making things up.

Earlier versions of some of this material have appeared in *New Economy*, *Sunday Business*, *Transmit* and *Tribune*. I wish to thank their editors for permission to draw on those contributions. I am also grateful to Spokesman Books for their patience and understanding. Michael Barratt Brown made many helpful suggestions which I have taken on board. I also owe a great deal to many professional friends and colleagues. Some of them are named in the references, but many must remain anonymous because I would not wish to embarrass them. Finally, the greatest debt of all is owed to Marianne Eva Reed who made an essential contribution to my work. Needless to say, the author alone is responsible for any views expressed.

Peter Reed

Introduction

Deregulation. Marketisation. Privatisation.
The jargon hardly trips off your tongue, but it well sums up the
doctrines guiding Tony Blair's proposed 'modernisation' of air
transport. Although the government is holding a formal policy
consultation[1], Blair has already made clear the kind of 'reforms' he
has in mind. If he succeeds in carrying these through, the resulting
changes could well prove irreversible, whatever their effects
eventually turn out to be. It is therefore imperative for mainstream
Labour throughout Europe to understand what Blair is trying to do,
assess the probable outcome, and ask in whose interests such policies
are likely to work. Here we focus on six representative issues –

● Air transport has grown up within a complex web of public
  enterprise, state regulation and international co-operation. Is it true
  that these 'shackles'[2] have effectively stifled the industry, and there
  can be no further progress until they are 'struck off'?

● Inspired by airline deregulation in the USA, the government has
  declared a 'general presumption' in favour of 'full liberalisation' of
  air services,[3] But does America really offer a successful model that
  we should strive to copy?

● Growing airport congestion creates a problem of how to allocate
  landing and take-off capacity ('slots'), but investing in extra runways
  leads in turn to serious environmental issues. Is the 'natural'
  solution[4] to these problems the maximum use of 'free markets'?

● Landing and take-off aids are part of a wider air traffic network
  which also faces severe problems of congestion, investment and
  safety. Is privatisation of that infrastructure[5] the best way of
  overcoming them?

● Tony Blair is pressing the rest of Europe[6] to share his faith in
  deregulation, marketisation and privatisation. Would an
  international aviation regime wholly based on these principles serve
  the best interests of airlines, employees, travellers and the wider
  population?

● The government appears to believe that its free market philosophy

1

is self-evidently true. Is there any theoretical or practical basis for such dogma or does the evidence suggest alternatives that work much better, and in the general interest?

Professor Alfred Kahn, the most prominent advocate of US deregulation, has rightly declared that aviation is the 'nearest thing we have in the social sciences to a laboratory experiment'.[7] The results of this experiment may also throw light on the dynamics of industrial competition, the forces driving globalisation, and the extent to which governments can influence these vast processes. Their significance thus extends far beyond the bounds of air transport. So let us test Blair's notions against the wealth of evidence now available.

Chapter One

Regulation:
Was Aviation Held Back by its 'Shackles'?

In a rare failure of vision, H G Wells did 'not think it at all probable that aeronautics will ever come into play as a serious modification of transport and communication.'[8] That was in 1902, just a year before the Wright Brothers achieved the first manned, controlled and powered flight in a heavier than air machine. Why did Wells prove so wrong? Popular histories tend to credit a series of heroic flyers and ingenious inventors. Like intrepid mountaineers, they conquered the sky 'because it was there'. An arbitrary selection would include names like Alcock and Brown, Leon Bleriot, Amy Johnson, Hugo Junkers, Charles Lindbergh and Igor Sikorsky. Their achievements were truly extraordinary. But the plain fact is, without government support, aviation could hardly have advanced beyond the wooden biplane.[9]

Where Does Technological Innovation Come From?

Aviation technology has always been stimulated by the public sector. Even in the USA, since 1915 the government has had a formative influence on both demand and supply of aircraft, military and civil.[10] It supports research, promotes advanced designs and encourages the transfer of military technology. For example, the first commercially successful jet transport, the Boeing 707, was developed out of a flight refuelling tanker for the B52 bomber. But US government support has gone much further, for example by sustaining manufacturers who lost out in civil aircraft markets. In recent times, these included such famous names as Douglas, McDonnell and Lockheed.

The Organisation for Economic Co-operation and Development (OECD), on the other hand, believes that innovation is 'driven by competition' between private firms. In its view, the role of government is confined to basic science, and building 'the coherent policies needed for innovation to flourish'. In a remarkable feat of ideological projection, OECD then illustrates this belief by contrasting a ricketty pioneering contraption with a picture of … *a Space Shuttle*.[11]

The Space Shuttle is just one part of a comprehensive effort by the

US National Aeronautics and Space Agency (NASA) to drive aviation technology forward. Its Advanced Subsonic Technology Programme embraces optical systems, composite structures, better engines and improved wing design. NASA is also developing novel concepts such as the Active Aeroelastic Wing in which entire wings act as control surfaces. The Agency's innovatory work extends to supersonic flight and air traffic control, but NASA is not the only source of technological dynamism. For instance, the Computerised Reservations Systems (CRS), which are revolutionising air transport, owe their origins to the US SAGE military early warning system.[12]

Of course, US manufacturers and airlines have invested large sums of their own to develop this public technology for commercial use. But technological uncertainty is anathema to private investors. That is why national governments have stimulated nearly all the basic technology – airframes, airports, avionics, engines and materials. They have also provided the infrastructure, physical and electronic, offered easy finance, developed operating procedures and, historically, even trained most of the pilots.

Has this vast public effort been successful? About the period 1925-1975, the leading US authorities on technology and economics conclude: 'Judged by almost any criterion of performance – growth in output, exports, productivity, or product innovation – the commercial aircraft industry must be considered a star performer in the American economy.'[13]

How Were Air Services Developed?

From the First World War onwards, aviation has primarily been driven by political contests between nation states, and between power blocs. Military demands have thus always been at the forefront. But governments have also required airlines to support national trade policies, maintain political lifelines and serve as public utilities. In fact, the majority of today's well-known airline 'brands' began as public enterprises or 'chosen instruments'. The USA is no exception. From an early stage, the US Post Office used mail contracts to build domestic air services, passenger as well as freight. The Army provided navigational aids. All this provided a secure basis for the development of both aircraft manufacturing and operation.

4

Over the years, the Americans have tried just about every way of supporting air operations.[14] During the 1920s, the Post Office had its own aircraft fleet, though lobbying by the US railways put an end to that. Successful public enterprise was then replaced by competitive bidding for mail contracts. This resulted in a disjointed jumble of franchised routes, which made it impossible for operators to build coherent networks. The Republican Hoover administration therefore instructed the biggest US airlines to *plan* a network. That is how American Airlines (AMR), TransWorld (TWA) and United Airlines (UAL) acquired their distinct east-west territories, while Eastern Airlines (EAL) served the Atlantic zone.

The 1932 New Deal administration viewed the Post Office contracts as an illegal conspiracy. They were accordingly scrapped, thus depriving the USA of air mail services. The Army tried to fill the vacuum, with disastrous results. After years of chaos, President Roosevelt was thus in 1938 obliged to set up the Civil Aeronautics Board (CAB). The CAB regime lasted forty years until the most recent act of deregulation. Throughout all these changes, the US Post Office and Navy helped to develop foreign operations, with Pan American (PanAm) in effect acting as an instrument of US foreign policy.

European governments were equally quick to spot the potential of aviation. Many of them sponsored 'flag' carriers. France was in the vanguard with lavish subsidies. Britain was somewhat more grudging in supporting its airlines. But during the 1920s and 1930s, UK governments swallowed their ideological prejudices, and took a progressively closer interest. They persuaded airlines to merge in return for subsidies. Other help included providing the services of RAF pilots. Despite this assistance, the two leading UK operators, British Airways and Imperial Airways, gradually slipped further behind their foreign rivals, as did the manufacturing industry. Just before World War Two, the Conservative government found itself with no option but to nationalise them. Thus originated the British Overseas Airways Corporation (BOAC).[15]

Why Did International Regulation Take A Bilateral Form?
In the 1930s, the UK held up PanAm's proposed trans-Atlantic services for two years, until a British operator could mount a

reciprocal operation. The Australians went one better and kept PanAm out altogether. The Americans could hardly complain because they had refused access to KLM and Lufthansa.[16] From an early stage. aviation thus began to develop in a way reminiscent of the old Navigation Acts in shipping, and for similar reasons.

After World War Two, the USA, having become the world's leading aviation power, pressed for a new approach. The Americans now had bases across the globe, a great aircraft fleet and a huge manufacturing industry. They perceived it in their interests to sweep away all controls. The USA argued for that policy at the 1944 Chicago Convention which established the post-war pattern of international air transport. But other countries were reluctant to submit to American power, and Britain proposed a world regulatory body. The compromise was Air Services Agreements (ASAs) negotiated between pairs of countries.[17]

Within these 'Bilaterals', the airlines flying between states mostly had to be controlled by nationals of the countries concerned. Those of other states were largely excluded. Such ASAs commonly specified airports used, number of operators, frequencies, capacity and tariffs. In case of dispute, both governments had to agree on solutions. Over the years, the treaties tended to become more detailed. In some cases, there was full 'predetermination' of traffic shares, which could sometimes be carried to great lengths. For example, where one carrier had bigger aircraft than another's, some of the former's seats might be 'roped off', i.e. deliberately left unsold. Such practices naturally led to criticism.

This was also true of the way tariffs were set. Within the bilateral treaties, individual airlines could not act unilaterally. Both ASA countries had to agree to a new fare – the 'double approval' principle. Most governments also insisted that tariffs had to be agreed between *all* the airlines in a given region – not just those serving routes between the two countries. For example, Belgian, Dutch and German airlines would take part in setting fares between London and Paris. Moreover, they often had a right of veto. These practices applied to services across the world.

Why So Much International Regulation And Co-operation?

The answer is that there was no alternative. By their very nature, international airlines form part of a network. A wide-bodied jet aircraft cannot land in a grass field: it requires a hard runway of a certain length and strength, together with elaborate communications and landing aids. So wherever that aircraft flies, there has to be prior agreement on infrastructure and operational procedures. Pilots need to talk to local air traffic controllers, so there also has to be a common language, which is English. Such matters have to be agreed between all states concerned. In this case, a United Nations agency, the International Civil Aviation Organisation (ICAO), sets operational and technical standards.

Similar logic applies to commercial activities. Suppose you travel from, say, London to Auckland, stopping off en route at Cairo, Delhi and Tokyo. In doing so, you may use several carriers, each with their own booking systems and currencies. The airlines make reservations, recognise each others' tickets, work out the overall fares, convert national currencies and share the proceeds on an agreed basis. These are highly complex processes. For example, the airlines were obliged to develop their own currency ('Fares Construction Units') in response to fluctuating exchange rates.

There has to be a clearing house to carry out such functions. This is the task of the International Air Transport Association (IATA). It is not too much to say that, if IATA had not existed, governments would have had to invent it. That is because a global system cannot work without some form of organisation. A network must have network fares and transfer arrangements. As for the fares agreed collectively at IATA, the airlines' decisions had to be approved by *all* the national governments affected by them. Despite a series of ideologically inspired attacks, IATA is still flourishing. Indeed it is gaining members. And even the current European Union regime permits airlines to set 'interline' fares at IATA.[18]

Did Classical Regulation Stifle The Aviation Industry?
Civil air transport began as a luxury transport service for aristocrats, film stars and millionaires. Now it is a routine mode of business travel and provides affordable flights for the masses. Traffic has steadily grown. Fares have consistently fallen. User choice has progressively been widened. Those regulatory shackles didn't prevent the emergence of turbo props, pure jets, wide bodied airframes, Computerised Reservations Systems or instrument landing systems. Neither were they able to suppress Inclusive Tours, Advanced

Booking Charters, APEX fares and a host of other popular facilities. Radical new kinds of airline like Britannia, Federal Express and South West came to the fore.

All these things happened under, indeed were nurtured by, classical regulation. Promising new operations were insulated from predatory attack. For example, the thriving British passenger charter sector grew up under such protection. A vital contribution was also made by consumer protection measures like Air Travel Organisers' Licensing (ATOL). Where operators fail, the ATOL guarantees that holiday makers will be brought home, and refunds secured. Significantly, all attempts to 'privatise' the ATOL system have failed. Public pressure has even brought about a tighter web of consumer protection.

The potential flexibility of classical regulation in the USA was demonstrated by Professor Kahn in a more dramatic way. As Chairman of the Civil Aeronautics Board, he led the abolition of all economic controls *before* the deregulation legislation came into force.[19] This was a silly policy, but Kahn did thereby prove, or rather rediscover, that there was no need to change the law to secure a much greater degree of competition, if desired.

There were similar possibilities for changing bilateral agreements and the IATA tariff mechanism. In the late seventies, for example, the UK began to 'freeze' excessively high fares.[20] This use of countervailing power proved highly effective, and the European Union 'competition' regime has come nowhere near matching its results. The Civil Aviation Authority also influenced IATA decisions at source, by the simple expedient of sending observers to tariff conferences. No system is perfect, and none of this is to argue for a return to traditional ways. But classical regulation offered plenty of scope for evolutionary change.

Thus we see that terms like 'shackles' are no more than ideological prejudice. This dynamic industry was not held back by its collective practices, by public support or by economic regulation. These were essential for its success. The development was an organic process.

● *Without the 'shackles' of public ownership, state regulation and airline co-operation, aviation could never have achieved anything like its present strength and diversity.*

- *Governments have played a vital role, often for military and strategic reasons, in developing aviation technology, and are still doing so.*
- *This has helped air transport to evolve from a luxury mode for aristocrats, film stars and millionaires into a routine business service and cheap travel provider for the masses.*
- *All institutions and policies need to move with the times, but the classical regulatory approach was well capable of being adapted to modern circumstances.*
- *It would thus be perfectly feasible to scrap outmoded nationalistic controls, while retaining the essential features of a managed regime working in the general interest.*
- *The case for 'striking off the shackles' therefore depends crucially upon some convincing proof that a Free Market can offer a demonstrably better performance.*

Chapter Two

Deregulation:
Does the USA Offer a Successful Model?

As well as routes, capacity and tariffs, air transport regulators also monitor the financial strength of airlines, their 'fitness' to operate and many aspects of safety. Imposing finance and fitness requirements, however, was felt by the American deregulators to discourage new entrants. These aspects were consequently watered down in the USA to the extent that 'an aspiring entrepreneur need only show that in a set of perfect circumstances the proposed operation could be feasible.'[21]

Safety comes under the Federal Aviation Administration (FAA), so it was out of the grasp of the free market enthusiasts who were put in control of the Civil Aeronautics Board in the mid-seventies. The Reagan administration at first favoured dropping safety regulation altogether. The argument was that it is 'irrational' for airlines to kill their passengers, because that would damage their competitive standing. Understandably, this argument did not much appeal to the US aviation community, and was quickly dropped.[22]

The main thrust of US deregulation was therefore to scrap all controls on routes, capacity and tariffs. Until the 1970s, free market economists had largely been ignored by people outside their classrooms. Then, with a change in the economic climate, politicians began to listen. In an era of 'stagflation', both Democrats and Republicans thought airline deregulation looked a winner. Bringing down airline prices would please travellers, discipline trade unions and help slow down inflation. Most airlines were unenthusiastic, although United saw an opportunity to expand at the expense of its smaller rivals. Free market enthusiasts painted such a glowing picture that the policy gained strong support right across the political spectrum. Consumer advocates like Ralph Nader joined in. The deregulatory tide became irresistible.

After a quarter of a century, it is fair to assess the results. It was claimed that unregulated competition would radically cut air fares, end discriminatory treatment of users, cut out wasteful frequency competition and over-lavish on-board hospitality, while vastly

Figure One (a) The Reduction in U.S. Air Fares Since Deregulation

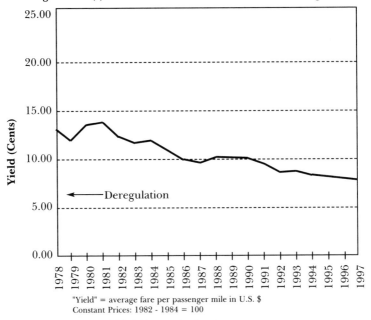

"Yield" = average fare per passenger mile in U.S. $
Constant Prices: 1982 - 1984 = 100

Source: Melvin A. Brenner Associates Inc.

As everyone agrees, average air fares in the U.S.A. came down after deregulation, while traffic went on increasing.

Figure One (b) The Growth of U.S. Air Traffic Since Deregulation

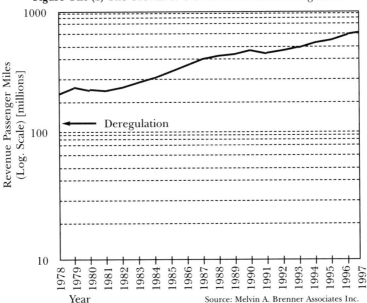

Source: Melvin A. Brenner Associates Inc.

improving service quality overall. These things would happen because the industry would be composed of a myriad, mainly small, operators, thus ensuring self-balancing competition, with 'rational' firms making 'normal' profits. There would be no 'bitter and extended price wars'. And Professor Kahn was particularly keen to 'nail' the fear that 'the big will eat the little.'[23] The USA would offer a brilliantly successful model to the rest of the world.[24]

Has American Deregulation Brought Down Air Fares?

Two of the strongest and most frequent claims for the deregulation of just about any industry are that it brings about much lower prices, and thus leads to a great stimulation of demand. Spectacular gains are claimed for the US airline version because fares on average ('yields') have come down markedly since 1978. It is also stressed that traffic has grown strongly since that time. The trends are shown in Figures One (a) and (b), reproduced by kind permission of Mel Brenner Associates. These diagrams are wholly uncontroversial. No-one, literally no-one, would question their basic accuracy.

Now look at the same trends in longer term perspective. The most cursory inspection of fares *before* de-regulation shows that they were heading steadily downwards for several decades under the Civil Aeronautics Board regime. There is, to put it conservatively, no evidence whatever that US domestic fares levels are generally lower than they *would have been* under traditional regulation. Figure Two clearly shows this.

However we rework the calculation, or jiggle the assumptions, similar results emerge. Mel Brenner's conclusion is relatively cautious. Another series shows that yields fell 2.5 per cent per year from 1950 to 1978, but sank at a *lower* rate of 1.9 per cent annually after 1978. If adjusted for fuel costs, which are outside the airlines' control, the figures become 2.7 per cent before deregulation, and 1.9 per cent after it. This makes no allowance for charters, common before 1978 but now almost extinct. Including them would reduce the pre deregulation figure still further.[25]

Even this is too cautious according to *official* US data. The Bureau of Labour Statistics includes an air travel component in its Consumer Price Index. This is a representative bundle of tariffs, corrected for

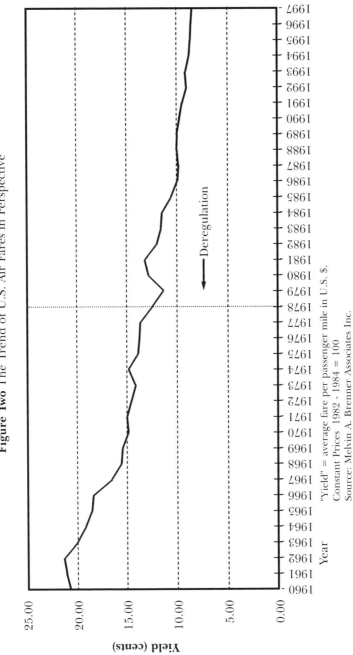

Figure Two The Trend of U.S. Air Fares in Perspective

"Yield" = average fare per passenger mile in U.S. $.
Constant Prices 1982 - 1984 = 100
Source: Melvin A. Brenner Associates Inc.

inflation and fuel prices. On that basis, the Bureau finds that US air fares, post deregulation, in general *rose substantially* in real terms.[26] This is probably going too far. Comparing tariffs is a very complex business, and it is essential to compare like with like. The official statistics may not adequately reflect a changing 'fares mix'. It is almost certainly true that captive users of 'full' fares are paying more than ever before. At the same time, however, fewer people are allowing themselves to be caught by such fares.

But whatever our qualifications, only one conclusion is possible: the Civil Aeronautics Board regime was highly successful in reducing air fares. To put it no higher, the post deregulation regime finds it hard to match the Board's performance. As Figure Three shows, the same is true of traffic growth. (Though here again we must be cautious because it is always possible to generate traffic with uneconomic fares.)

Our picture is very much at odds with prevailing ideological messages, but the truth can be found buried in official 'small print', at least in Britain. As the Civil Aviation Authority puts it: 'the principal driver of changes in passenger demand is changes in gross domestic product ... [the] main determinant of growth will continue to be the rate of growth of GDP and of consumer expenditure ... the major factors affecting air fares are ... changes to oil prices and other aircraft operating costs ...' Consistently with this, the Civil Aviation Authority honestly adds that 'liberalisation in Europe is expected to have only a modest effect.'[27]

We should note that just about all the former British nationalised industries show a similar long term trend in costs and prices. Privatisation is claimed to be a success on the basis of the same Statistical Myopia, i.e. by starting the calculation from a carefully chosen date.

While free market economists generally ignore the mounting evidence, some people try to explain the revealed facts by giving the credit to technology.[28] (This sits uneasily with the claim that the Civil Aeronautics Board regime was rigid and undynamic.) Was the impact of technology greater before deregulation than after it?

Over the last few decades, there have been big advances in propulsion technology, (increased range, lower fuel consumption and reduced operating costs), in airframe design (weight savings and increased payload), in control techniques (better operational

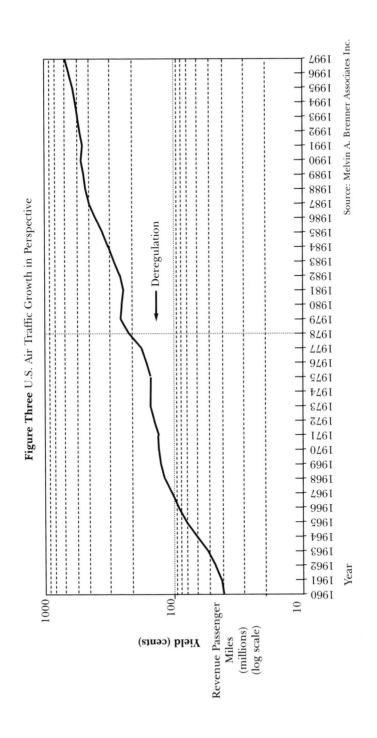

Figure Three U.S. Air Traffic Growth in Perspective

Yield (cents)

Deregulation

Revenue Passenger Miles (millions) (log scale)

Year

Source: Melvin A. Brenner Associates Inc.

performance and less flight crew), and in aspects such as Computerised Reservations Systems, yield control etc. Although the ageing of the US aircraft fleet will have affected the take-up rate, the technology argument thus lacks credibility.

It is also fallacious, even in its own terms. Technology does indeed reduce operating costs, but we must ask: who benefits from those reductions? And by what mechanism? Under Civil Aeronautics Board regulation, the airlines reaped but modest profits while passengers enjoyed the long term trend to lower fares. In other words, the carriers demonstrably failed to capture most of the fruits of technology. It could therefore only have been the regulators who ensured that passengers shared in the benefits, as opposed to all spoils going to shareholders.

It is also worth noting that classical regulation was flexible enough to allow the commercial rivalry between airlines to express itself in a rapid take-up of new technology.[29] For example, Pan Am placed the initial orders for the wide bodied Boeing 747. As a result, TWA feared being left behind in trans-Atlantic competition. American Airlines then joined in because it faced TWA on US coast-to-coast routes. This happened under both US domestic and trans-Atlantic regulation. Such competition may not have been entirely rational; that is a different issue. But it could, and did, happen under classical regulation.

Does Competition Squeeze Out Discrimination Between Different Users?

Throughout transport history, few issues have aroused so much emotion as when users of the same facilities have been treated differently. That is why, when *laissez faire* was approaching its mid-nineteenth century climax, Britain was imposing ever tighter regulation on canals and railways. Tariffs were controlled; facilities had to be 'reasonable'; and 'undue discrimination' was outlawed.[30] There were independent regulators to police all this, because Victorian governments had no illusions that competition alone could protect rail users – even with more than a hundred rival operators.

In the USA, the Civil Aeronautics Board took a similar view. Although it would put as many airlines on routes as it thought feasible, the Board set fares on a mileage basis. These were based on average costs for the whole industry. Operators could offer 'promotional' fares up to fifty per cent below the standard tariff. If airlines made excessive profits, the Board would even things up by adding other, less profitable, destinations to those airlines' networks. Whatever its faults, this approach was universally judged to be fair. It also ensured that smaller communities were connected to the network. More than 500 such towns enjoyed that accessibility. Under deregulation, a third have lost their services.[31]

Many free market economists would view this loss as leading to improved resource allocation. Under deregulation, they used to argue, fares would be more closely related to costs. If some points were uneconomic to serve: it was right to drop them. And short haul passengers had been subsidised by those on long trips. Market forces would ensure that what travellers paid would closely reflect the costs of carrying them.

The reality is that US fares are now discriminatory in the extreme. A snapshot may reveal passengers from St. Louis to San Diego paying less than those between St Louis and Chattanooga – one quarter the distance. Or the cheapest Cincinnati and Houston routeing may be through Newark – a detour of some 1,000 miles. These examples will almost certainly be out of date because every day sees tens of thousands of fares changes. During a fares war, there may be hundreds of thousands of such revisions. The sole constant is that passengers using certain airports pay two or three times more than those using others. Most inflammatory of all, travellers may find that they've paid many times more than people sitting next to them, for exactly the same service.[32] How on earth can this happen?

One reason is the use of 'yield management' in order to 'charge whatever the market will bear'. Airlines work out how many seats to allocate to low fare traffic, and how many to keep back for business travellers. The latter book at much shorter notice. The capacity thus allocated ('seat inventories') may vary by route, day and timing. Today, you can have a $9.99 fare. Strangely, it may be sold out – however quickly you try to book. You will then be offered other fares. In truth, there may only have been a dozen or so of the bargain tickets. Such cheap tickets may also have restrictions, such as minimum length of stay, designed to put off business travellers.

None of this was supposed to happen under deregulation. Even if there were few competitors on a given route, the mere possibility of new entry was supposed to keep things in order. This was the theory of 'contestable markets'. It has proved wholly mistaken. Now a fall back argument is becoming popular: such discrimination doesn't matter. Only wealthy businesses suffer; and they can afford to pay. Again this is wrong. Big companies use their power to squeeze special deals out of the airlines. It is small business, and families travelling at short notice, who are thus 'caught'; or people who live in the 'wrong' areas. Discrimination now reigns supreme.

Does Free Competition Stimulate Higher Service Quality?

Under the Civil Aeronautics Board, it was argued, airlines provided too much capacity, and their cabin service was far too lavish. Competition would ensure that users could choose whatever mix of price and quality they wished to pay for. But alongside this 'tailoring' of supply, there would be an across the board improvement in standards at every level. For is it not axiomatic that, to prosper under competition, private firms *have* to satisfy their customers?

This is a complex issue, and we must be sure to compare like with like. Business users demand short notice booking, travel flexibility, frequency and on board comfort. These are expensive features. They help explain the cost differences between, say, British Airways and specialised 'low fare', or charter, operators, like Britannia or easyJet. To avoid turning away high fare, late arriving business users, scheduled airlines tend to 'overbook'. For every such 100 seats sold, on average perhaps 85 people will actually fly. In this case, an airline may sell up to 117 tickets in order to fill those 100 seats. But occasionally more than 100 people may turn up at the check-in desk In such cases, those people denied a seat are entitled to 'Denied Boarding Compensation' (DBC).

On the other hand, the main priority of 'Leisure' passengers, the main source of long term traffic growth, is low fares. Specialised airlines set out to meet that requirement. They do not aim to provide the same on-board standards or service range as British Airways. As with the British low fare scheduled operators, they may primarily serve secondary airports. Carriers like BA also offer low fare facilities in their 'back cabins', with corresponding service standards. These take such forms as Advance Purchase, Stand-by and Part-charter tariffs, or 'Special Promotions'.[33]

An important function of Yield Control is to avoid the danger that business travellers may find ways of using cheap tickets. More than anything else, airlines fear 'commoditisation'. That is where ticket sales become part of a 'spot' market, and suppliers have no control over their prices. Airlines thus consider it a vital interest to keep right out of the kind of market favoured by Professor Kahn. To counter this threat, airlines like British Airways create expensive 'brands' like Club World, with wider seats, leg rests, and interactive videos – at appropriate fares. The idea is to achieve similar brand loyalty to that enjoyed by, say, chocolate manufacturers. These firms can change the colour, shape and size of their wrappers in order to disguise price increases. Incidentally, the more competitive the US chocolate industry became, the more the price of chocolate ('candy') bars went up.[34]

Any comparisons of service quality over time must take account of these commercial factors. But after all such allowances, a clear trend emerges. In the USA, the quality trend is unmistakably downwards. On-board meals have almost disappeared. Cabin crews have been reduced to legal minima. Routeings are increasingly circuitous: one analyst even talks of 'hubbing and spoking for ever, without reaching your destination'.[35] Aircraft changes are frequent; airport delays widespread; connections often missed; baggage too often lost. 41 per cent of users, in a recent survey, have experienced this decline. Another survey of service quality ranks most American carriers well below their foreign rivals. All this despite marketing costs being some fifty per cent higher than before deregulation. Add to this, the oldest aircraft fleet in the developed world, and a clear picture emerges.[36]

The US government is reluctant to admit shortcomings because it wishes to export the American deregulation model. Even so, the Department of Transport Inspector General admits that the US industry is doing little about the 'most deep-seated underlying cause of most customer dissatisfaction' – flight delays and cancellations. Astonishingly, Denied Boarding Compensation has not been increased at all during the last quarter century.[37] So much for the pressure of competition!

No surprise that Ralph Nader, once so enthusiastic about

deregulation, has helped form a broad coalition of users and politicians to demand 'fundamental reforms'.[38] Nader's shopping list is lengthy. It includes more aircraft leg room, 'prohibiting holding of passengers on airliners parked on the tarmac for unreasonable periods', and 'uniform and formal service standards'. Nader clearly no longer thinks that competition will deliver these basic travel requirements.

How Could The Dinosaurs Survive Without CAB Protection?

Free market economists confidently predicted that the famous old carriers like American, Delta and United, would be fortunate even to survive. As there were supposedly no economies of size, they would probably share the fate of the dinosaurs. The conditions were ideal for small new entrants: a surplus of experienced labour, easy finance and aviation authorities eager to help newcomers. The 36 regulated operators of 1978 were joined by almost 200 new carriers.

Well over three quarters of those original new entrants have now disappeared. Most of the rest have commercial agreements with the major airlines, i.e. they 'feed' traffic to and/or use the identifier codes of the Majors – another important source of consumer dissatisfaction. ('Majors' are airlines with annual revenues of more that $1 billion.) The three biggest operators, American, Delta and United, now carry between them more than sixty per cent of US domestic traffic. If the currently proposed mergers go through, four vast groups, American/TWA, Delta, North West/Continental and United/US Airways, will control nearly ninety per cent of that traffic.

These are truly MegaCarriers.

Far from balanced free market competition, this has been a typical capitalist elimination contest, played out at historically breakneck speed. Economic orthodoxy cannot explain the process. For that, we must turn to the political economy of Marx, Schumpeter and Kalecki. The US industry is on the way to a structure like that in motor cars or soft drinks, with two or three dominant firms.

The same trend is now global with great 'Alliances', such as American Airlines/British Airways, ('One World'), and Lufthansa/ United Airlines ('Star Alliance') to mention only a few leading players. There can be no doubt that, once unhampered by the nationality clauses in bilateral agreements, world aviation will rapidly become dominated by no more than half a dozen gigantic combinations. So what form does the competitive struggle actually take?

The great old airlines refused to accept the fate that Professor Kahn and his colleagues had assigned to them. They expanded to gain 'critical mass', seized control of infrastructure and fought for strategic power over route networks. When the initial post-deregulation shake out was over, the Majors were seen to have some compelling advantages. These include: (a) extensive hub-and-spokes networks which allow them to 'steer' traffic and dominate particular airports; (b) control of airport terminals, gates and 'slots'; (c) ownership of Computerised Reservations Systems (CRS); (d) great influence over the retail trade including, where necessary, large commission payments; (e) the ability to mount attractive loyalty ('Frequent Flyer') schemes; (f) well-established 'brand' images; and not least (g) the ability to attract able managers.

The Majors draw on all these strengths to manage their capacity and pricing with pin-point selectivity, according to the competition they face in specific markets.[39] They have invested huge sums in developing Computerised Reservations Systems to a point where they have a dominant position in the retail trade. Travel agents sell the flights they can most conveniently look up on their videoscreens, because that saves time. If fares and retail commissions are identical, a timing shown on the top line of the first display will be sold in preference to one lower down, or on the second or third screen. Display position can have a massive impact on ticket sales.

Naturally, an airline which has spent billions on Computerised Reservations Systems will not favour the timings of its rivals at the expense of its own. Disputes have therefore arisen about display bias, and regulatory rules have been made governing such displays. These are becoming more detailed in the way they specify how flights, connections and tariffs should be set out. But new tricks are being thought up all the time. For example, airlines in an Alliance may share the code for a through service, even though at least two different operators are used. Apart from deceiving users, this device enables the Computerised Reservations Systems provider to list a flight three times, once for each airline and as a joint service. This uses up display space, and pushes rivals' services off the first screen.

There is no foreseeable limit to the ability of MegaCarriers to harness Information Technology. For example, five US Majors have now collectively founded Orbitz, an Internet retailer with exclusive rights to their cheapest tickets. (This development has, inevitably, attracted the attention of the Department of Justice which carries the anti-trust torch.) One airline is going so far as to auction seats over the Internet at prices below those at which the operator itself sells.

The pace of advance is such that there is a running battle of wits between Computerised Reservations Systems owners and legislators as each ingenious new technique for bias comes in.[40] This is leading to another extraordinary contradiction. In the name of fostering market forces, a plethora of detailed rules is creating a degree of regulatory intervention hitherto unseen – or even thought about. The logic is thus driving Computerised Reservations Systems towards becoming a public utility.

So What Happened To All Those Dynamic New Entrepreneurs?

This CRS capability enables the Majors to deal with any smaller rivals on a highly selective basis. In recent years, there has been a constant stream of hopeful newcomers. At a certain stage in the industry cycle, they can find experienced managers and aircrew at pay rates well below those of the Majors. Aircraft are also usually available at bargain prices. And the authorities like to give these newcomers special help, for example by insisting they have access to Computerised Reservations Systems on 'non-discriminatory' terms. Because these small newcomers depend upon otherwise unemployed resources, however, there are built-in limits to their growth. In particular, any expansion by the Majors would quickly attract their pilots to much better paid jobs.

Those small airlines which have been successful have stayed inside a 'niche' – low fare services between secondary airports, regional or feeder operations, charters and so on. The example of PeoplExpress (PE) is instructive. It began as a no frills/low fare carrier. From an unfashionable base in Newark, PeoplExpress served airports a little off the beaten track, thus avoiding 'nose to nose' competition with the Majors. Reservations methods were simple and passenger service somewhat basic. There were no unions, no middle management and extraordinary workforce flexibility. The atmosphere was something like that of a cult. The resulting low fares were aimed at people using buses and cars. It was brilliantly successful … for a time.

And then, the fatal mistake. People Express launched a frontal attack on American, North West and United. PE believed that, with costs at half the Majors' levels, it had nothing to fear. Having previously ignored the upstart, the Majors used their full Computerised Reservations Systems power to protect their high yield traffic. They matched PE's fares in their back cabins. They put on more frequencies. The Majors already had services which were vastly superior in terms of connections, on-board service and influence over the travel trade.[41] When PeoplExpress tried to expand westwards, it had an equally rough ride. Continental even offered free 'Sympathy Lunches' to people in PE's check-in queues. PeoplExpress was doomed.

Professor Kahn blamed PE's failure on 'pin point' predation. But this is almost impossible to prevent under Competition Law, as interpreted in the USA. What law were the Majors breaking by simply matching a competitor's prices? Uniform prices, contrary to the prevailing orthodoxy, are usually a sign of strong competition. The plain fact is that, after decades of contemplation, the Americans can't even *define* the term airline 'predation'. The US authorities' only recourse is informally to twist the arms of the Majors, and plead with them to 'stop it!'

Classical regulators could simply disallow, or limit, any fares thought to be not in the public interest. Where airlines achieve ultra low costs by legitimate means, they may well deserve protection. But in the competitive jungle, as boxing commentator W. Barrington Dalby used to say, 'a good big'un will always beat a good little'un.'

Did The Corporate Raiders Inject Some Economic Rationality Into US Aviation?

Another kind of new entrant produced more lasting results. After deregulation, some US airlines attracted hostile take over bids, in the form of Leveraged Buy Outs (LBOs). Financiers would buy carriers, using bank loans in the form of high interest 'Junk Bonds'. The resulting huge debt was supposed to inspire managers to heroic feats of cost cutting and business efficiency.[42] The new owners had no interest in airline strategy or public service; their eyes were fixed on cash flow. If there were higher profits from breaking up airlines, then assets would be stripped. As one Wall Street observer said, this took 'the same view of the corporation as the praying mantis does of her mate.'[43] Free market economists, on the other hand, would see this process as putting assets to more productive use, and thus applaud it.

No operator was safe. Continental Airlines (CAL) is perhaps the most spectacular case. From his base at Texas International Airlines (TIA), Frank Lorenzo, who features in an examination of 'corporate pirates and robber barons in the cockpit'[44], took over the much larger operator. As a result, the merged entity found itself with long term debt of $642 million, but equity of only $142 million. Continental's (then) chief executive pointed out that 'the operating profit required to service this debt is more than our two companies together have ever earned.' He then committed suicide in his office.

Within two years, Continental had engineered its own bankruptcy ('Chapter 11') in order to scrap its labour contracts. The subsequent strike was broken when CAL's pilots were promised a profit sharing scheme. Later the profits were 'upstreamed' to the Texas International holding company – so there was nothing available to share. Aircraft were transferred to a non union subsidiary. New staff were taken on at much lower pay.[45]

The process was repeated at other companies, including a (then failing) PeoplExpress and Eastern Airlines. EAL was stripped of assets, including aircraft, its Computerised Reservations Systems and terminal infrastructure. These were transferred to other subsidiaries at less than market value. Since then, Eastern has evaporated. Continental went bankrupt a second time. The Texas International empire has disappeared. No matter: according to free market theory, resources have been soundly allocated, by being put to more profitable use.

The legacy of the junk bond era is still very strong. Famous names like North West, TWA and United all fell victim to raiders from outside the industry. North West Airlines, with one of the industry's strongest balance sheets, traditionally had scarcely any debt. As such, it was an attractive target. After the Leveraged Buy Out, the airline was saddled with more than $3 billion of debt. The debt:equity ratio was an incredible 30:1. Despite subsidies from Minnesota state, North West fell into crisis. It was rescued in co-operation with its trade unions. The employees traded pay cuts and work concessions for a 33 per cent equity stake. United was rescued in the same way, and it is a remarkable fact that the world's biggest airline is now majority owned by its employees.

The workers at these airlines have 'sold' part of their earnings to save their jobs and win some influence over company decisions. It isn't yet clear how this will work out. In operational matters, there is no doubt that, for perhaps the first time, employees are being listened to, with fruitful results.[46] Unions and management, however, may take different views on such issues as the affordability of wage increases. Despite the employee ownership stake, significant problems have thus not yet been ironed out. But this great experiment deserves close study.

All this has happened in a generally bleak climate for American wage earners. Starting from 1979, and continuing until the mid-nineties, the *real* hourly pay of most of them was severely eroded. This was true of the lowest paid 80 per cent of men, the three-quarters of the labour force without a college degree, low-wage women workers, blue-collar employees, and every kind of new entrant to the labour force. Families tried to offset the downward pressures on their real wages by working longer hours. The typical American is now working two weeks more than twenty years ago. These trends were to some extent reversed by the upturn of the late nineties. But it is clearly a myth that increased freedom for market forces has been an unmixed blessing for the majority of Americans, many of whom are hardly better off now than at the end of the 1970s.[47]

Because US air transport is highly unionised, established employees have been able to maintain their earnings and conditions reasonably well. Most pressure has been on new recruits who often work for significantly less pay than their colleagues – the 'two tier' approach. With several years of expansion, the industrial climate is becoming tense, with unions fighting for 'snapbacks', i.e. trying to regain past losses. Whether they can achieve this will depend upon the industry regaining some financial strength – a somewhat distant prospect.

Has Deregulation Created A Smoothly Adjusting, Self-Balancing Free Market?

Under Civil Aeronautics Board regulation, the industry's route structure formed a lattice grid, as shown schematically in Figure Four. There was easy passenger interchange ('interlining') between the company systems and operating staff were known to offer unbiased advice to travellers. Most airlines connected a series of points to form a linear pattern, often facing several competitors. This structure was expected to collapse after deregulation. Free market theorists expected a myriad small airlines to flourish, presumably operating on a point to point basis. By definition, therefore, the operational map would have been highly fragmented. It would have become much more difficult for people living outside big cities to travel around the USA.

Nothing remotely like this happened. After the initial upheaval of the late seventies, the surviving airlines were seen to have changed their route systems. They had become a series of overlapping bicycle wheels, as shown schematically in Figure Five. The 'spokes' connect thousands of city pairs through so-called 'Fortress Hubs.' Most services, including those of 'captive' airlines, are timed through these hub airports to permit connections. The objective is to maximise control over traffic. Each US Major has one to four such hubs. Most of them are dominated by a single carrier. From these fortresses, the rival Majors attack each other by pushing new spokes into alien territory.

Even in such a highly simplified illustration, we can see that travellers from a number of points will have a choice of flying with either Airline A or B. In each case, they will be channelled through to the airline's Fortress Hub, where they will often have to change aircraft.

The competition between the Majors themselves, at least until now, has been a far from smooth process. Partly that is because of the broad tendency of capitalist competition to generate over production and surplus capacity, to which aviation is no exception. Historically, these capacity surpluses have been eliminated by economic depressions.[48] Air transport also has its own specific features which exacerbate the problem and lead to serious instability. These are structural in nature and not, as free market economists allege, a result of 'irrational management'.

Where there are alternative services, business demand can be influenced by small timing differences, particularly on short flights, and the number of services flown. Frequency thus has a disproportionate influence on demand.[49] No carrier can afford to offer less frequency than its rivals. But once a flight is scheduled, the extra cost of filling empty seats on the aircraft is very small: perhaps no more

Figure Four U.S. Airline Point-to-Point Route Structures under CAB Regulation

Airline A ●·······● (Base)

Airline B ●————● (Base)

NB. This is a schematic diagram showing two airlines. In practice, some routes would have more operators

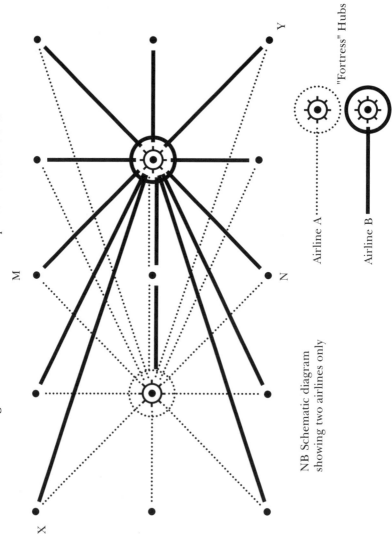

Figure Five U.S. Airline Hub-with-Spokes Route Structures

X

M

N

Y

NB Schematic diagram
showing two airlines only

Airline A ·············

Airline B ──────

"Fortress" Hubs

than on-board refreshment, sales commission, etc. This could be as low as one per cent of fully allocated per seat costs. As the product 'perishes' once the aircraft takes off, operators may try to dispose of unsold seats in any way they can. This explains the proliferation of amazing bargains and, in Europe, the existence of 'bucket' shops.[50]

Carrier rivalry can become particularly intense if one of them invades another's 'primary' routes, which are profitable on the basis of fully allocated costs. Suppose that, to start with, only Airline A links points X and Y through spokes via its Fortress Hub. At this stage, Airline A's fares are based on its full costs. Airline B then adds a spoke to its network which allows it also to operate between X and Y over its own Fortress Hub. As a newcomer to that through service, Airline B may well cost its own product on a 'marginal' basis. Airline A will, accordingly, have to reduce its own prices in order to keep its traffic.

Or suppose that Airline A uses some of its surplus equipment by opening a direct service between Points M and N around the rim of its network. Airline B, funnelling M-N traffic through its hub, will thus face a superior product. It will accordingly price down to retain its traffic. If it wishes to stay on that direct route, Airline A will probably be obliged to match, thus losing any hope of covering its own full costs. In this way, instantaneous fare cuts may radiate further across the complex web of interlocking hub and spokes systems in the entire USA.

The Major airlines have no option but to behave in this way, for they are locked into the immense costs of operating their hubs. Because all their flights are timed to interconnect, this leads to airport congestion and low equipment utilisation. The need to compete on frequency also leads to 'downsizing' of aircraft, which means higher unit costs. Most of these costs can't be scaled down if revenue falls. (Neither do they rise proportionately if traffic increases.) Because of this 'gearing' effect, airlines can swing rapidly from profit into loss, and vice versa. Quite small changes in demand can have a dramatic effect upon profits.

As well as a regular profit/loss cycle, we also observe a continuing long term 'yield erosion'.[51] As surplus capacity is always being generated, and marginal cost competition always breaking out, costs and fares are always being ratcheted down. Even after an airline has gone bankrupt, the sale of its assets may realise less than the cash that flows in from continuing to operate. As a result, failing airlines usually struggle on and on. This exacerbates the fares wars. The airlines' efforts to avoid them, for instance by using Computerised Reservations Systems to 'signal' price changes in advance, have been ruled illegal. In the absence of regulation or airline collusion, there is no solution.

The extraordinary truth is well stated by the (then) President of American Airlines in the industry's own economics text: 'The very nature of scheduled air transport ... dictates that supply and demand, even in the best of times, will be severely out of balance.'[52]

A Healthy And Profitable Industry?

Free Market theory failed to predict any of this, and cannot explain the US industry's predicament. In a capitalist economy, the prime test of success is profitability. On these terms, US deregulation is an abject failure. Over the long term, US manufacturing has averaged net profits of between 4 and 6 per cent. In the twenty pre-deregulation years, airline net profits averaged 2.8 per cent. For the ten post-deregulation years, they were 0.5 per cent. Add in 1988-95, and the average falls to 0.3 per cent.[53] Since then, the industry has enjoyed several prosperous years, but it now faces a catastrophic loss of profitability. If the US authorities applied traditional British standards of 'financial fitness', some famous airlines would be put out of business – immediately.

After full allowance for cyclical effects, the American situation is getting steadily worse. This is reflected in the industry's credit ratings, and it makes it hard to raise capital for much needed fleet renewals. As a consequence, the US airlines' balance sheets are saddled with enormous debt – by the mid-nineties, more than 65 per cent of their capital.[54] Wall Street accordingly rates the debt of virtually every US Major airline as 'speculative' or 'junk'.[55]

As many airlines can no longer finance equipment with internal revenue, there is a great deal of leasing. Indeed, about half the US fleet is owned by leasing companies. But despite the lavish federal aid promised by George W Bush following the New York terrorist attacks, the financial outlook is not bright. It has been pointed out that, to restore Wall Street's confidence, 'the required operating margins are well above any historical performance and the required new equity actually exceeds the total market capitalisation of these companies.'[56]

Where will the process end? There will no doubt be cyclical ups and downs, and lavish help from the US government.[57] But the profitless competition will probably go on indefinitely. The conventional managerial response is to demand yet more sacrifices from the work force. However, the repeated bouts of cost re-structuring will offer only a temporary respite. Once *all* competitors are down at new lower cost levels, the downward spiral will begin all over again. The imperative question is: how to fill the excess capacity thrown up by the inherent nature of the competitive process? Or how, in the first place, to stop it arising?

Surely Deregulation MUST Have Achieved Some Successes?

Successes are hard to find. Even the most publicised cases, like the Dallas-based South West Airlines (SWA), support that verdict. SWA is a superbly managed operation with high density, short haul, routes forming linear structures. It offers a basic product with simple tariffs. Because there is no hubbing, the airline enjoys quick turnrounds and low labour costs. The latter is not due to lower wages. American Airlines, another Dallas based carrier, has a labour cost per passenger of more than two and a half times that of South West, but staff earnings don't vary much between the two carriers.[58]

The difference is SWA's astounding productivity. It isn't achieved by grinding the work force: with 84 per cent of its staff in trade unions, South West is one of the world's most highly unionised airlines. A clue is American's fleet of nine aircraft types and thirty three crew qualifications. The corresponding figures for South West are one and two. A basically simple operation is carried on in an atmosphere of genuine participation – noticeably absent in European attempts to copy the model.[59] But we must not overlook South West's success in winning exemption from local airport traffic distribution rules. The airline operates from a home base in downtown Dallas, from which other airlines are excluded.[60]

Does the future belong to airlines like South West? Could the

MegaCarriers really be dinosaurs? Will Professor Kahn prove right after all?

South West regards itself as a 'niche' carrier, carrying point to point traffic on dense routes. Perhaps a fifth of the overall US traffic is suitable for this mode of operation. That leaves the Majors with their endemic problems. Competitive pressures make it difficult for them to escape from their hub and spoke structures, and the huge inefficiencies these impose. And yet, almost everyone in the US industry knows that the system 'which Europe and the rest of the world seem ready to copy in fact creates great inefficiency while harming or inconveniencing almost everyone in sight, and costs the American people billions in excess fares.'[61]

Nowhere have such policies worked. According to the Civil Aviation Authority, the 'most dramatic developments' were in Australia. 'The single new entrant, Compass Airlines, which was helped by a government decision instructing Ansett and Australian to provide the new entrant with gates, ceased operations after one year. It was later revived. But a second time, it quickly disappeared.' Since then, Ansett has been grounded because of maintenance deficiencies. Recently it was liquidated.[62] This led to such acute capacity shortage that Korean Air was invited to provide internal services for Australia.[63] It is difficult to overstate the significance of this; there are few, if any, precedents.

Meanwhile, after failing under private ownership, Air New Zealand has been renationalised. In Canada, according to the Civil Aviation Authority, the 'post-liberalisation market seems to be dominated by two major airlines with little immediate prospect of new competition.' Since then, Canada has found itself with but a single carrier.[64]

The European Union regime amounts to deregulation (although EU officials avoid that term). EU airlines can now operate within, and between, other member countries. They can also 'establish' themselves in any member country. This has improved operational flexibility and has led to some modest, but worthwhile, economic gains. What it hasn't done is tackle the main problem, which is that certain European fares are clearly too high. The main complaint has always been the disparity between 'on-demand', i.e. business fares and the low fares 'at the back end'.[65] Between the main European airports where traffic is heaviest, there is little sign that 'competition' is having any effect. The facts are set out in a European Commission (EC) publication which complains about the 'contradictory and unsatisfactory trend concerning fares.' Apparently, 'while promotional fares have become more widespread, the prices of fully flexible fares have increased.' Furthermore, the 'proliferation of tariffs, the availability of seats at the most publicised promotional fare ... [and other factors] make it harder for consumers to compare competing offers.'[66] As we would also expect, there has also been a decrease in the number of direct flights with the growth in hubbing.[67]

The standard apologia for these disappointing results highlights the emergence of the new low fare airlines. But low fare operations had been developing for many decades, for example charters, excursion fares and APEX tickets. As pointed out earlier, most traffic growth is now of this type. The regulatory space to allow these operations was negotiated before the Eurpean Union was even in the picture.[68] The airports used tend to be at secondary points, and not frequented by major carriers. In fact, most of them would have been available under the old bilateral treaties. This is a welcome development, but it has little to do with EU deregulation; it is a continuation of the long term growth in low fare traffic. The 1970s Labour government showed how to deal effectively with indefensibly high air fares. Under the EU regime, this ground has effectively been lost. Experience is clear that countervailing power, wielded by specialist regulators, is the best way of defending users' interests. Unlike the free market, a managed regime actually works.

The facts are clear. Almost none of the benefits claimed for deregulation – in fares trends, discrimination between users, service quality, even company profits – have been realised, and the US industry is more concentrated than ever. And this, let us stress, is the *fourth* bout of US airline deregulation.[69] The results are always pretty much the same. Even after World War Two, when easy public loans enabled 3,600 (sic) new entrepreneurs to enter the industry, only a handful could survive, and then only as 'supplemental' (charter) carriers. In the face of this mountain of evidence, those who persist with free market dogma remind us of the television sketch in which a learned Professor explains, with the help of higher mathematics, that he has proved it will never rain again. As the raindrops fall, the sodden Professor doggedly repeats his prediction, and keeps on doing so long after his mumbo jumbo has been washed right off the blackboard.

When will Tony Blair notice the rain?

● *Professor Kahn's experiment has produced clear results: US airline deregulation has failed to deliver on almost any of its promises.*

● *Its performance on fares trends is inferior to that of the former Civil Aeronautics Board regime, while discrimination between users has risen to unacceptable levels, and service standards continue to fall.*

● *The US industry is in an unstable, unprofitable and unhappy state, with little hope of solving its problems because they are structural in nature.*

● *The possible cures, public or private regulation, the latter stemming from even greater industry concentration, are politically very difficult to administer.*

● *There is no significant evidence from anywhere outside the USA running counter to these conclusions.*

● *There are certainly features of the American industrial scene which deserve close study, but no real evidence to support Tony Blair's faith in 'full liberalisation'.*

Chapter Three

Marketisation: The 'Natural' Solution for Airport Congestion, Capacity Shortage and Environmental Pollution?

After nearly ten years of deregulation, the European Commission has failed to achieve some of its major air transport objectives. Predictably, the suggested remedy is 'more competition' but this shows few signs of working. In any case, runway congestion makes it almost impossible for new competitors to obtain enough airport 'slots' to start up viable services. (The new low fare operators have, so far, wisely shunned head-on competition with their bigger rivals; it remains to be seen whether they will avoid the mistakes of their predecessors, such as Laker and PeoplExpress.) A 1993 EU Regulation[70] was designed to 'open up' the congested airports. It has had no such effect. The Regulation was scheduled to be revised by 1997. A somewhat anodyne revision was proposed in 2001.[71]

There has been such a long silence from Brussels because the slot problem is not readily amenable to free market treatment. According to the theory, congestion is simply due to an excess of demand over supply. It should be dealt with by raising prices 'until markets are cleared'. If those markets don't work smoothly, there needs to be more competition. If that isn't possible, then entrepreneurs should be 'incentivised' to increase the supply of capacity. No need to worry about the environment, because the proper use of markets can deal with any problems there. How is all this supposed to work?

What Is The 'Slot' Problem?
A slot is a planned timing for an aircraft movement, either for take-off or landing, in or out of a specific airport. As well as runway capacity, slots are closely bound up with the use of flight approach paths, taxiways, aircraft stands, and passenger terminals. At any busy airport, decisions have to be taken on which operator gets what timings.

Traditionally, a key role has been played by 'Grandfather Rights' which meant that airlines had customary rights to slots they already operated. The rest of the slots were allocated by horse trading between carriers. Regulators didn't intervene because the process worked smoothly, and there were few complaints. To carry out this process, every large airport had a scheduling committee of airline representatives.

Their deliberations ranged far beyond the airports at which they were based. Allocating slots is a complex process because it has to mesh together the various international networks. Each schedule has to take account of time zones, differing night noise rules at airports around the world, and commercial requirements. Many services therefore have to be threaded through narrow 'time windows' in various countries. An international scheduling conference, convened by IATA, brings together the airline representatives who have real time access to their computers back home.[72] Then follows a great deal of bargaining and fine tuning.

The trouble is that no slot allocation system, however sophisticated, can overcome an acute shortage of runway capacity. The pressure to get into airports that are already full is constantly growing, and cannot be met. For example, London's Heathrow (LHR) has irresistible attractions for scheduled operators. That is because of the geographical spread, frequency and interconnectivity of Heathrow's air services. So someone has to decide priorities, and ration access.

The traditional IATA method is now ruled out because, as a 'concerted practice', it is said to infringe the Rome Treaty. That is why 'non-discriminatory' and impersonal rules to allocate slots have been designed at EU level. They are applied by 'airport co-ordinators'. In Britain, as we would expect, the function has been privatised, and is carried out by a company owned by British airlines. The government claims to have no influence over this company.

Before EU deregulation, slots were needed only by airlines which had won route licences, but the latter have now been abolished. As the Civil Aviation Authority points out, airport co-ordinators are, as a consequence, faced by slot requests 'ranging from the wildly speculative to the cut and dried.'[73] At one time, CAA regulators would have thrown out frivolous and hopeless applications. But that is no longer permitted. Such decisions are strictly for markets.

So far as *vacant* slots are concerned, the current EU Regulation gives some priority to 'new entrants'. But few airlines are prepared to give up any of the slots they currently hold. Why should they? Neither are they enthusiastic about losing Grandfather Rights and, by exerting political pressure, have so far managed to retain the principle. Such rights are, of course, wholly incompatible with any version of a free market. Such a market would feature a redistribution of slots and some kind of auction process.

The current European Union rules fall far short of this. They lay down broad priorities, such as favouring scheduled over charter operations. But after they have been fully applied, there is usually still a queue of unsatisfied customers demanding slots. The Civil Aviation Authority suggested a way out of the impasse: a 'further and unequivocal test ... [which] should not require the co-ordinator or anyone else to make a subjective choice.' CAA's solution was that: 'the easiest and least controversial solution would seem to be for the selection to be determined by lot.'[74] No doubt, slot allocation could then be entrusted to Camelot or Ladbrokes.

Can Free Markets Solve The Slots Problem?

At the time this idea was floated, the Civil Aviation Authority's (then) leaders were well aware of operational realities, and didn't really believe that a pure market approach would work. Wholly unburdened by practical worries, the Office of Fair Trading (OFT) asserts that the sale of slots between airlines is 'a natural and pro-competitive method' for allocating scarce runway capacity.[75] OFT also apparently believes that 'without sale, there are no obvious criteria for the allocation of slots.'[76] Airlines should thus be charged 'market' prices which vary with the pressure of demand. Some operators would be prepared to pay such peak prices; others would be 'priced away'. Has OFT cracked the problem?

First, how 'natural' is the buying and selling of slots? The Conservative government tried hard to apply market thinking but the issue proved more complex than anticipated. Instead of those beautifully simple blackboard curves of demand and supply, a thorough consultants' analysis resulted in 300 pages of detailed organisational logic.[77] Sadly, the 'Free Market' option fell at the very first hurdle. Undeterred, the (then) government insisted on testing a 'Market Hybrid'. This retained as many features of a market as was thought feasible.

The conclusion was that slot trading would require *three* (sic!) levels of administration, reflecting the extreme complexity of the task. It could also have led to a trebling of airport charges and a ten per cent increase in fares. This would have affected all airlines flying into Heathrow, not simply those of the European Union.

The basic reason why wholesale slot trading proved so 'unnatural' is that airline networks cannot be treated like a 'spot' market for potatoes. As pointed out above, Heathrow timings have to be compatible with the slots that airlines hold at the other ends of routes, and at intermediate points. They form part of an intertwined complex of routes, frequencies and networks. That is why the system cannot work at all without international scheduling conferences. Imposing a simplistic market has been shown to lead to costly, unwieldy and bureaucratic mechanisms which defeat the whole purpose of the exercise.

The ruling ideological principle is that governments should simply lay down ground rules, and not judge the claims of rival carriers. Only the market should decide priorities. But, in real life, the inescapable fact is that someone *has* to make judgements between rival airlines and services. It has never been easy, but the Civil Aviation Authority showed how to use public hearings to make broadly based decisions. Although no longer allowed to allocate slots between UK airlines *within* Britain, the Civil Aviation Authority has been called upon to do just that between British airlines at *Tokyo*.[78]

If slot trading is hardly 'natural', is the Office of Fair Trading's approach at least 'pro-competitive'? It is important to note that charges for slots would not generally be passed on to individual groups of travellers.[79] They would be absorbed across entire networks, particularly by foreign airlines. British carriers, with a much greater proportion of their services at congested airports such as Heathrow and Gatwick, could thus be at a big disadvantage. Moreover, other governments would certainly retaliate by charging British operators for slots.

As major network operators can absorb such charges more easily than small carriers with limited resources, a 'free' market for slots would accelerate the strong forces towards airline concentration. Moreover, with unregulated slot trading, American carriers could undoubtedly price most British airlines right out of the London slots 'market'. The reality is that the Office of Fair Trading's approach could hardly be more *anti*-competitive, and designed to hurt British interests. Selling slots to the highest bidder would lead to a Heathrow largely monopolised by wide bodied aircraft, like Boeing 747s, primarily operated by MegaCarriers, and serving long haul destinations. It could squeeze out the short distance routes they didn't want, and many of the smaller airlines providing them. To some extent, this is already happening: Inverness, Liverpool and Plymouth have lost their connections to Heathrow's network.[80] Other British cities will no doubt follow. As the fragmented private rail industry is incapable of substituting direct high speed surface links, the overall value of the network to UK passengers and freight shippers would be diminished.

Even more remarkable is the Office of Fair Trading's view that slots are the property of the airlines holding them. But airlines invariably hold slots because they were awarded operating rights by governments. They didn't buy them. As already noted, the majority of today's profitable routes were built up under regulatory protection, or with public support. No surprise that OFT also believes that, if the authorities substitute one operator for another, or open markets to competition, they should compensate the 'losers'.[81]

Others may judge that, if anyone makes money out slot trading, it ought to be the taxpayers who made it all possible. Or perhaps the workers whose jobs may be lost as their employers sell their holdings, or draw the wrong number in a game of Slot Bingo.

Is There Insufficient Competition Between London's Airports?

All these misjudgements flow out of the same *a priori* reasoning that shaped the policy of US airline deregulation. Nowhere does the Office of Fair Trading even attempt to provide *evidence* that its approach can produce the results it assumes. It confines itself to dogmatic assertions. This is typical of the government's approach to a wide range of airport problems. A classic example was a hurried exercise into whether the London system, owned by the privatised BAA plc, should be split into three separate, rival airports at Heathrow, Gatwick and Stansted.

The operational reality is that National Air Traffic Services (NATS) operate London's airspace as one unified complex. All three airports (and others such as City and Luton) are located inside the same block of controlled airspace, the London Terminal Manoeuvring Area

(TMA). Within that crowded rectangle, arriving aircraft are marshalled for descent, while those taking off are kept safely apart from all the others.

So interwoven are these flight patterns that take-offs and landings at one London airport closely interact with movements at the others. This is also true of the non-BAA airports. For such reasons, the most efficient pattern of airspace use would be for each London airport to serve different geographical areas. This would reduce conflicting aircraft movements. If all westbound traffic used Heathrow, all eastbound used Gatwick, and so on, it would thus greatly increase Terminal Manoeuvring Area capacity. This is known as 'sectorisation'.

There would be little point in 'competition' unless the different London airports each served the widest possible range of destinations, or at least had a significant overlap. In this case, Gatwick, Heathrow and Stansted airports would each have flight paths radiating in all directions. That would greatly increase the number of conflicting movements. It would thereby markedly reduce London's airspace capacity and probably increase the chance of 'near misses'.

Free market economists, oblivious to the wastes of competition, might well regard such losses of capacity as a price worth paying. But there is another awkward reality. As already noted, literally every major scheduled airline is anxious to base its UK services at Heathrow, and nowhere else. This despite Heathrow's operational handicaps: a cramped site, scattered terminals, poor surface connections, and severe night limitations. But all that aircraft 'stacking', taxiway queuing and passenger 'bussing' is outweighed by the rich nexus of frequencies and interconnectivity. For airlines, this makes Heathrow an irresistible attraction.

This operational complex cannot easily be split up, or its traffic diverted elsewhere. Heathrow is bursting at the seams, but 'overflow' traffic shifts to the other London airports only with great reluctance. Much of it would simply move to the continent rather than divert to UK regional airports.[82] The 1970s Labour government tried to solve the problem by means of Traffic Distribution Rules (TDRs). These specified the routes and carriers allowed into each London airport, and were based on elaborate technical studies.[83] (The EU regime allows Traffic Distribution Rules if they are 'non-discriminatory'.)

The policy was hard to apply because foreign airlines, and their governments, strongly resisted being moved out of Heathrow. A compromise policy directed 'new' operators into Gatwick, while Stansted was to be an 'expansion chamber.' Mrs. Thatcher scrapped all this without putting anything in its place. Everything was henceforth to be decided by 'market forces'. Naturally the outcome was even greater pressure on Heathrow. Given their head, market forces would produce One Colossal Heathrow. For obvious reasons, this is impossible.

These facts of life have already compelled the government to drop the idea of splitting up the London airport system.[84] Undeterred by this setback, the Civil Aviation Authority then made a deliciously silly proposal for making the terminals *within* those airports compete with each other. This is akin to promoting competition between the various rail platforms at Paddington or Victoria. Naturally, this idea too was quickly shot down, on operational grounds.[85]

The interests owning London's prime airports have somewhat more worldly aims. The ever-increasing demand for access to Heathrow and Gatwick, pressing on limited capacity, creates a potential for astronomical profits and rents. On revenue of £2,261 million, the former British Airports Authority (now BAA plc) enjoys an operating surplus of £615 million.[86] In selling off BAA, Mrs Thatcher created a privatised hyper-monopoly. That is because many international airlines have literally no alternative but to use that airport, and to do so at specific times.

Does The 'More Commercial' Approach Benefit Airlines And Travellers?

BAA has been quick to exploit every commercial opportunity offered by its monopoly status. Indeed, Heathrow is a star turn in marketing text books as 'one of the most attractive segments for retailing and for producers of luxury and fashion brands'.[87] As a model 'captive' market, with every imaginable device to channel people into shops and restaurants, BAA is regarded as a 'retail stock play'.[88]

Within reason, such amenities may enhance the travel experience, but there comes a point where the main purpose risks being lost to sight. Airports are transport terminals, not shopping malls. On one famous occasion, operators were driven into a fury by a campaign by an airport to encourage local (non-travelling) week-end shoppers. Check-in, security and lounge facilities now compete for space with boutiques, jewellers and fish restaurants. To some extent, the airlines can exert countervailing power, but their pressure for stronger regulation speaks for itself.[89]

While airlines can fight their corner, no-one effectively speaks up for 'captive' passengers. The logical end point of present trends is for most public facilities – lounges, seats, toilets etc. – to be phased out altogether, so that passengers are compelled to use those in airport shops and restaurants. This is where a powerful user body could exert much influence. The existing Air Transport Users' Council[90] has never carried enough weight. Given the failure of 'market forces' to protect consumers, a statutory body is essential. It should have enough powers, backed by research capability, to make a nuisance of itself.

In the face of the evidence, Blair's consultation paper claims that the UK has 'benefited' from 'a more commercial approach to airport management'.[91] Just four paragraphs later, however, it compares London unfavourably with the continental airports which have built runway capacity well ahead of demand. BAA's more 'commercial' approach has apparently led to demand, as the government puts it, being 'frustrated.'[92] It has also generated a barrage of complaints about the quality of service to airlines.[93]

Ever since its privatisation, BAA has dismissed suggestions that any additional runway capacity is required in London. Way back in 1989, the Civil Aviation Authority pointed out that an extra London runway would be needed by 2000.[94] BAA found this 'disingenuous'.[95] The present saturation of both Heathrow and Gatwick clearly shows who was right on this. The result, as British airlines point out,[96] is that London is steadily losing ground to airports such as Amsterdam, Frankfurt and Paris. A comparison with Paris is particularly revealing. Charles de Gaulle airport is setting out its stall for the new era of hub and spoke competition, as seen in America.[97]

As with US deregulation, although hub and spokes networks make little sense from the travellers' point of view, airlines are forced into it by the need to survive in competition. Connect 20 origins and 20 destinations through a hub and one airline can serve 440 different markets. Waves of arrivals and departures can be timed to connect, say, every two hours, linking all points on the route system. Such intensely 'peaked' operations make great demands on infrastructure at particular times. A delay to one flight can ripple through the whole day's operations. At Paris, however, the right conditions have been created for Air France to operate six interconnecting 'banks', with up to 40 to 50 arrivals and departures.[98] An overstretched Heathrow simply cannot match that.

Such a performance is feasible because French airport capacity has been planned to increase well ahead of demand. While London is reluctant to expand, Paris has built two extra runways at Charles de Gaulle, making four in all. (Heathrow has two full length runways.) Paris has also built additional terminals, with direct links to the ultra-high speed rail network. These achievements are possible because French public bodies work towards agreed long term strategic objectives.

Can Private Airports Be 'Incentivised' To Provide Extra Capacity?

Contrast the Paris situation with London where runway congestion has reached crisis proportions.[99] Under the present approach, however, the government is not directly involved in airport provision. Investment projects can only be initiated by airport owners. Naturally, private firms will only invest if guaranteed a commercial return. BAA is sometimes accused by local residents of plotting to build more runways at Heathrow and Gatwick, but that would be against its financial interests. To maximise its profits, the company needs to fill up its existing capacity, like that at Stansted, before installing any more in the London region.

Given private ownership, the government sees no other way than to 'incentivise' BAA to carry out the necessary investments, i.e. guarantee the company bigger profits from doing so. This can be attempted because airport charges are regulated by the Civil Aviation Authority, in tandem with the Competition Commission. Maximum charges are based on the Retail Price Index, minus a certain percentage – the familiar 'RPI – X' formula. This is applied to average revenues per passenger.

BAA's maximum permitted charges are currently based on its total revenues (the 'Single Till' approach), including property, franchise and retail income. These non-aviation takings account for some forty per cent of the total, so including them in the figures keeps down the payments made by airlines. The regulatory aim has been to allow BAA to earn a 'reasonable' return on its investments. This included an allowance towards new capital projects, such as the proposed Heathrow Fifth Terminal. Thus it was hoped to keep the extraction of 'rents' from airlines within the bounds of decency, while encouraging BAA to expand capacity as required.

This is far from the supposed ideal of 'market clearing' prices. Existing airport charges do not price away 'marginal' operations until demand is balanced with supply. (According to free market economists, that is why the slots problem exists!) Neither do those charges 'signal' the need for expansion projects. According to the orthodoxy, regulators are therefore to blame if airport profits are channelled into real estate rather than into building more London runways. In the bargain, incentives are lacking to offer airlines an acceptable quality of service.[100] The answer, according to the Civil Aviation Authority, is thus to *increase* BAA's profits to 'encourage investment.'[101]

How can that be done? First, by excluding property and retail income from the 'regulated asset base' (the 'Dual Till' approach). From there, it is a logical step to 'market clearing' prices for runway use. But at that point... *hesitation!!!* CAA admits that 'while market clearing prices may provide good signals of where new capacity is desired, they may not provide good incentives to actually deliver it at the socially desirable time ... because ... the airport may earn better returns through ongoing exploitation of current scarcity than it would by expanding capacity and thereby reducing the scarcity rents.'[102]

So, after racking up those charges, the market may not work after all. Private capital may still chase the highest returns wherever they are to be found. CAA's conclusion? Allow Heathrow and Gatwick charges to rise *part way* towards market clearing levels.[103] Why not all the way? Here reality breaks in with a reference to practical difficulties. Not least amongst these is American opposition to higher charges.[104]

The airlines' response has also been less than enthusiastic. While BAA's non-aviation revenues will be wholly 'freed', Heathrow airport charges may go up by no less than forty per cent.[105] Such price rises, the Civil Aviation Authority admits, will 'transfer economic rents' away from airlines, and thus raise airport profits. But even after this hefty price rise, no-one knows if BAA will use its higher profits to expand capacity or whether 'it would be more likely to use substitutable space in the terminals for aeronautical or commercial activities.'[106] Will the private owners squeeze security and check-in space to pack in more boutiques and cocktail bars? CAA doesn't know, but it is clear that the 'airport must retain ultimate discretion over and accountability for strategic direction.'[107]

It would be hard to find a purer example of ideologically driven thinking. But policies must be judged by how they work in practice. Have previous policies worked any better?

As British Airways says, there is 'an intensifying airport capacity crisis in south east England'. Privatisation has a lot to do with that. But it would be wrong to overlook the contribution of governments to London's problems over the years. There have been many studies, inquiries and consultations, but little action. Governments have shied away from tough decisions. They prefer 'salami' tactics: expand by stealth, while doing just enough to dampen the opposition of local residents. Exacerbated by privatisation, this approach cannot deal with a situation where the number of Heathrow passengers is expected to double by the year 2020.[108]

Can Free Markets Be Reconciled With The Environment?

In the face of such a huge predicted increase in traffic, some environmentalists argue for a 'cap' on the maximum number of flights permitted. Tony Blair, so strongly wedded to free markets, would hardly agree to that. But literally any government would hesitate to apply such a limit, given the immense contribution of aviation to economic growth, exports and employment.[109] Unilateral action by individual states is, in any case, hardly feasible.

This is not to say that movement limits are operationally impractical. Not long ago, Heathrow had such a limit, but it was scrapped as soon as the figure was reached.[110] Moreover, when circumstances require, governments have been ready to cut down the number of flights. Even the Americans have done so, both on US domestic routes and the North Atlantic. The most remarkable case arose out of the 1981 US air traffic dispute, when Reagan had striking controllers led away in chains. For some years, the authorities ran a makeshift air traffic control system, using a fraction of the previous labour force. Capacity in some cases was almost halved but, as Figure Three shows, there was little effect on airline traffic. Because there was less congestion, service quality actually improved. Air travel was hardly disrupted at all.[111]

Such experiences throw into relief the tremendous wastes of deregulation. In principle, there is much scope for limiting aircraft movements, without adversely affecting passengers or freight. In a rational world, this would be an important aim. In practical terms, the political and commercial barriers are formidable. So how does the government propose to deal with the environmental problems of airport expansion?

The Civil Aviation Authority is clear that 'taking direct account of these externalities is not one of its statutory objectives as economic regulator'. That 'is the role of the planning system', i.e. what used to be known as 'town and country planning'.[112] So much for integrated transport policy! Meanwhile the government is looking for ways of speeding up the inquiry process, In doing so, it appears to be seeking ways of shifting powers of decision from local authorities towards private business interests. So how does this square with a claim that 'decisions on airport development will be made by Ministers in light of *all* the factors'.[113]

In the past, such decisions have been taken with the help of Cost Benefit Analysis (CBA). This has been used to bring 'externalities', like the impact of air noise on local residents, into the same evaluation as the costs and revenues of airport operation. Unfortunately, Cost Benefit Analysis lost much credibility in the seventies because economists tried to measure *all* such effects in terms of cash. In simulating free markets, questions were posed like: 'how much would you pay to get rid of this nuisance?' or 'what is it worth to you to avoid being killed?' Noise, for example, was assessed by its adverse effect on house prices. Affluent areas were thus found to suffer more than low income districts. The apogee of this approach was the Third London Airport Enquiry of 1971 ('the Roskill Report') which tackled such issues with breathtaking ingenuity.[114] Unfortunately, however, its policy conclusions were acceptable to neither the Heath nor Wilson governments.

Rejecting the marketisation of Cost Benefit Analysis does not mean discarding it altogether. Neither does it exclude a role for money because many components, such as building costs, have to be assessed that way. But it makes little sense to measure 'intangibles' like noise, visual intrusion or damage to archaeological sites in simple cash terms. Each element should be treated in whatever terms are most appropriate. This leaves a vital role for social judgements. Systematic ways of doing this exist, and are well tested.[115] They should be used.

At this point, it would be wrong not to give the government credit for proposing to judge airport projects by a new set of objectives. These are 'accessibility', 'economy', 'environment', 'integration' and 'safety'. Despite professional criticism[116], the new approach is a clear step forward. It will help to identify 'three or four' London expansion possibilities, for public consultation. The government will thus set the policy context. But then, it is back to market forces: 'investment in additional airport capacity will be undertaken by operators and investors according to commercial criteria.'[117]

The trouble is that private firms take little interest in pollution unless it affects their financial results. The government therefore believes that those who cause pollution should 'cover the costs'. It is 'particularly keen to develop the use of economic instruments'.[118] What this could mean is shown in a special appendix to the consultation paper.[119] Therein we are told 'It is often necessary to establish a price mechanism', but this is difficult because of the 'lack of well-defined property rights ... [which] prevents the existence of a market for external effects'. Naturally, the 'ideal solution is to establish property rights. It will then be possible to find out individuals' willingness to pay for marginal reductions in aircraft noise.'[120] This will show how much that polluters should pay for the relevant environmental costs to be 'covered'.

Sometimes, we can agree, this approach could make sense. A text book case would be a factory belching out noxious fumes. It might be possible to work out the resulting costs of cleaning up the surrounding area. Local people, for example, could be compensated by the factory for their dirty washing. Everyone would thus be no worse off than before. External costs would be 'covered'. In the same way, it is argued, a market could be created for, say, airport noise. In aid of this, the consultative paper claims, for example, that the noise damage costs of an Airbus A310 are £34 per landing or take off.[121]

Although it is hard to take such precise figures seriously, the idea of compensation for local residents is worth exploring. An official committee[122] suggested a levy on passengers to fund improvements around the airports. But as the Civil Aviation Authority points out, much of BAA's financial surplus is in the nature of rent: it is the fruit of *socially* created demand. As such, interests other than BAA's shareholders have legitimate claims upon it. Local residents bear the brunt of air nuisance, and a levy on airport profits would help to compensate them. This would be fully consistent with the principle of 'polluters pay'. (The extent of the perceived injustice can be measured against the £2 billion compensation recently suggested for Heathrow residents by the European Court, but the legal process is far from over.)

Under present policies, however, no-one is satisfied with the situation, apart from BAA's shareholders. None of the government's suggestions confront the basic structural problems of London's airports. The stubborn fact is that airport privatisation makes it almost impossible to reconcile some seriously conflicting objectives. For example, compare London with Manchester. Like Paris, Manchester airport has installed capacity ahead of demand. It has achieved commercial success while, at the same time, showing concern for regional development. Its local government ownership ensures that the interests of residents can be taken into account.[123] The various strands of policy are thus integrated. In London, in contrast, there is a basic conflict of interest.

As a result of the policies followed, Heathrow is steadily losing ground to continental rivals, such as Amsterdam, Frankfurt and Paris. Neither is London, despite its historic strength, well positioned for the future. Ideal locations for a leading pan-European hub are places like Munich, Vienna and Zurich. London is too peripheral. As the European Union develops, British operators will tend to shift their commercial emphasis to central Europe, and this is already tending to happen. British Airways has a continental foothold, British Midland is in alliance with Lufthansa, and Air UK is now owned by KLM.

BA's partner, American Airlines, showed what can happen in this kind of economic climate. In the 1970s, AMR shifted its headquarters from New York to Dallas – broadly equivalent to moving from London to Moscow. Such moves are becoming easier because airlines can already base certain functions in almost any part of the world. Seat reservations, revenue accounting and yield control are obvious examples. This is just the beginning. Obsolescence can strike quickly at transport infrastructure, as the former London docks so graphically prove.

As global citizens, we may see a great deal in favour of such trends, particularly where they help less developed countries. But it is far from clear that decisions based solely on company profits will work in the best interests of the British, or any other, economy. How will Mr. Blair tackle this problem? The government will be publishing an airports consultation paper, but it has already provided some clues about its thinking. It will come as no surprise that the Civil Aviation Authority believes that the case for favouring interlining is 'not clear'.[124] But the government has anyway 'little scope' in these matters 'since much depends on carriers' commercial policies.'[125]

This is fully consistent with the prevailing orthodoxy that whether airlines switch their main bases away from London or not, is a matter for 'market forces.' Of course, substantial 'local' point-to-point traffic would still flow between Britain and various continental hubs. But the industrial centre of gravity – headquarters, bases, support functions – could well transfer away. Air transport, and aviation-related jobs, many of them high quality, could well be lost. There would be adverse effects on the wider British economy. Too bad if it happens, because UK policy is firmly based on giving market forces their head.

Consistent with its free market outlook, it looks as if the government will content itself with indicating where it believes airport expansion is acceptable, and leave the rest to the market. Is there no alternative to this passive stance?

An alternative course would be to engage in some strategic thinking.

For example, one option would be closer integration of Heathrow, Gatwick and the other airports in the London region. This would require high speed train connections between those airports, and also with those like Birmingham and Manchester. An integrated national system could offer big advantages to users. It would not be ideal for airlines: British Airways claim that splitting its network between Gatwick and Heathrow inflates its costs by half a billion pounds per annum.[126] This approach would also share out between residents of several areas the environmental pain from traffic expansion.

Another possible strategy might be a wholly new 'green field' development, perhaps an estuarial or off-shore site. The aim would be to shift the entire Heathrow living operational nexus en bloc, as far as possible away from people. Such a 'virgin' site would allow air operations, surface access and environmental effects to be optimised from the beginning. Eurpean Union Traffic Distribution Rules would allow such a strategy if it was 'non-discriminatory'. A target date could be set for a wholesale transfer, say, ten or fifteen years into the future. All interests, including local residents and nature conservationists, would thus be given a fair opportunity to adapt to changed circumstances.

What about the required investment finance? Unlike flying itself, airport ownership is extraordinarily profitable. That is why there is so much clamour for privatisation. But private owners serve no economic purpose. All they do is cream off rents which should properly go to the community. If the project in question was, say, a new theme park, the 'entrepreneurs' behind it would acquire in secret as much of the required land as they could. Their objective would not merely be land for the airport itself: they would aim to capture as much as possible of the increased land values generated in the surrounding region. The lion's share of planning gain ought to go to the community.[127]

At one time, British public enterprises contributed massive sums to the Treasury. A new, publicly owned, London airport would be able to do the same. Moreover, it would have the resources properly to compensate any local residents affected by nuisance. It could also afford effective measures to protect historic sites and the natural environment. Several European Union countries are looking into such 'environmental' airports. It is not our intention to argue for any particular option, but to stress the need for strategic airport planning. Such planning is commonplace in such bastions of free enterprise as Colorado and Texas. Why is it beyond 'New' Labour?

Can Marketisation Solve The Problem of Global Warming?

Strategic airport planning may help to reduce pollution at regional level. But it cannot do much to counter the global warming which, according to the UN Intergovernmental Panel on Climate Change, is a grave threat to the stability of the biosphere, and thus to all life on earth.[128] This view of the situation is shared by the US National Academy of Sciences.[129] Moreover, the (combined) US National Academies have recently drawn attention to 'strong evidence' that, in the past, 'major and widespread climatic changes have occurred with startling speed'.[130] They also point out that 'Physical, ecological and human systems are imperfectly understood, complex, non linear and dynamic. Current changes in climate are predicting conditions ... outside the range of recent historic experience.'[131]

Although aircraft emissions play a small (though growing) role[132] in climate change, this problem must be taken very seriously. What is the government's response?

It is to frame the problem in terms of market transactions. For example, we are told that a Boeing 747-400 imposes an average 'marginal damage cost' of £18.49 per long haul passenger or $2.88 per thousand passenger kilometres. Increasing fares by 6 per cent, it is claimed, would 'cover' these costs. This would reduce travel by some 5 per cent. Market equilibrium could thus be achieved, and environmental costs 'covered'.[133]

But the problem isn't to 'cover' the costs of these destructive processes. So far as practicable, it is to eliminate them. Tony Blair's approach does no more than trivialise some of the gravest problems facing humankind.

Whereas scientists admit they do not fully understand these processes, orthodox economists do not shrink from constructing 'markets' in global warming. Such calculations are being taken much further in the USA where they have been used by George W Bush to justify his refusal to sign up to the Kyoto treaty. William Nordhaus, for example, has a computer model purporting to show that the costs of halting global warming would be some ten times the benefits.[134] As usual with such models, the conclusions are built into the starting assumptions. Literally any 'interference' with free markets will, by definition, lead to everyone being worse off. No surprise that the ecological models of mainstream scientists come to wholly different results.[135] But the natural scientists also stress that there are complex relationships which they cannot measure. For example, there 'are few convincing attempts to assess the value to society of the loss of [ecological] resilience' which provides 'insurance' against the uncertain environmental effects of economic growth.[136]

As hard as we try, it is difficult to see how such problems can be solved with the aid of market incentives. The government favours 'voluntary' agreements, perhaps with quota trading. The trouble is that commercial aviation will never agree voluntarily to any measures which it finds financially painful. The likely reaction is well shown by the way the European Commission was obliged to withdraw its attempt to phase out 'hush kitted' aircraft.[137] These relatively ancient vehicles cannot meet modern noise emission standards, but the USA, in particular, strongly opposed their elimination. That was because of severe pressure from American operators, manufacturers and used equipment dealers who feared that such aircraft would become unsalable in Europe. The European Commission accordingly backed down.[138]

Given substantial public support for research and development, it may be possible to agree with the industry on stiff environmental standards for *future* aircraft types. But it is naïve to expect airlines to be enthusiastic about painful sacrifices in their current fleets. Neither do tradable quotas offer much hope of progress. The MegaCarriers, particularly the Americans, would hope to buy the quotas of smaller airlines and of the developing countries. This is what happened with slot trading in the USA.

There may well be a useful role for such economic incentives, but this ought to be in support of direct measures. For the only effective way to cut down aircraft emissions is to control them at source. That means stepping up the current international efforts to set more exacting standards on aircraft emissions, and to enforce them. The political barriers to serious action are daunting, but that is no excuse for not trying. And in doing so, we should never lose sight of the fundamental point made by the Royal Commission on Environmental Pollution: 'Deregulation of the airline industry in the USA ... had damaging effects upon the environment. It led to the use of smaller aircraft and lower load factors, and thus to an increase in emissions per passenger kilometre.'[139]

'New' Labour should listen to voices like this. The official dogmas may help to justify huge private monopoly profits, but they are incapable of throwing light on such complex problems as runway congestion, airport expansion and environmental pollution. The present approach will never work, and is threatening the future of the industry. The free market economists who advocate 'natural' solutions remind us of the elderly male virgins who give moral advice on birth control to mothers of large families. What the situation demands is realistic thinking, strategic planning and political leadership of the highest order.

- *Far from being 'natural', the application of simplistic 'free market' notions to problems like runway congestion leads to artificial, expensive and unworkable schemes.*
- *London's airports are part of one highly complex system and major decisions on their future must be taken on a system wide basis, while taking proper account of the interests of airlines, users, UK regions and the wider population.*
- *Airport privatisation, reliance on 'market forces' and the abdication of public responsibility for airport development are major reasons for declining service standards and a London capacity shortage of crisis proportions.*
- *Even government officials admit that 'incentivising' private business to expand airport capacity may not work, although well aware it will result in even more spectacular profits and rents for the privatised hyper monopoly.*
- *These problems will remain unsolved until the government confronts the real structural issues, develops a long term strategy based on the public interest, and works to emulate the successes of French planning.*
- *The environmental dangers call for tough decisions by courageous political leaders rather than yet another flirtation with 'markets', and Tony Blair's approach does no more than trivialise some of the gravest problems facing Humankind.*

Chapter Four

Privatisation:
Creating a Railtrack in the Sky?

Experience with airports clearly refutes any notion that private is better than public in the running of complex infrastructure systems. No doubt, a Labour transport spokesperson had this in mind when declaring that 'Our Air Is Not For Sale!' In due course, the very same politician, later a Treasury Minister, played a leading part in selling off 'Our Air'. What could have prompted such a spectacular change of mind?

Why Privatise A Successful Public Enterprise?
National Air Traffic Services used to be part of the Civil Aviation Authority which integrated several key functions, including economic and safety regulation. Because of the close interaction between civil and military airspace, NATS was jointly operated by CAA and RAF personnel. It has three main tasks (a) tower operations, controlling landing, take off and taxiway movements at certain major airports, (b) approach control, again at major airports, the most important being the London Terminal Manoeuvring Area (mentioned earlier), and (c) the *en route* tracks ('airways'), or other controlled airspace, through which aircraft are routed and kept safely apart.

Of these, the *en route* function is by far the most commercially significant. Airspace control has always been regarded as a 'natural' monopoly, although it will come as no surprise to learn that ways are being sought to make some airways 'compete' with each other.[140]

Under public ownership NATS built a world reputation as an effective, efficient and safe provider of infrastructure. It has an outstanding record of increasing productivity, reducing air navigation charges, improving service and enhancing air safety. While doing that, it has usually shown a tidy profit. Why should anyone want to interfere with such a successful operation? Blair argued that privatisation would (i) allow management to mount international operations; (ii) inject some 'private sector dynamism'; and (iii) permit the raising of badly needed private investment capital. At the same time, he claimed, safety would be the overriding priority.[141]

These proposals met stiff opposition from air traffic controllers, airline pilots and others. Most remarkably of all, the British airlines, united on a policy issue for the first ever time, also opposed 'a sale which was based upon a commercial rate of return'. It was less surprising that the airlines also felt that 'overseas activities should only take place when domestic service was well provided for.'[142] So nobody outside the official camp took Blair's arguments seriously. Why was that?

(i) There may well come a time when, under the European Union Single Sky proposals[143], NATS could perhaps take over some continental airspace. It may prove technically possible to do that from Britain. But no legal or structural barriers prevented NATS from expanding abroad. The actual constraint wasn't public ownership. It was the refusal of governments to allow a publicly owned NATS to look overseas.[144]

(ii) As for private sector dynamism, this is scarcely in evidence, for example, with buses (outside London) or railways, both of which are in steady decline. Ever since Dr Beeching, there has been a steady inflow of private business people to the public sector. Their record speaks for itself. Most of them were wholly unprepared for, and unable to adapt to, a world immeasurably more complex than that of private business. What always tended to confuse them was the wide range of objectives set for public enterprise, as opposed to a simple chase for profit.[145]

(iii)The arguments about private finance are based on long standing Treasury orthodoxy. They bear little resemblance to the ideas Labour put forward in opposition. It may therefore be useful to trace the evolution of thinking on Public/Private Partnerships (PPP).

Are There Advantages In Using Private Capital For Public Projects?

In its original form, Labour's version of Public/Private Partnerships[146] was quite different from the Conservatives' Private Finance Initiative (PFI). Shadow Ministers were well aware of the huge backlog in public investment, and how difficult it would be to make this up quickly. Because of the anticipated pressure on public funds, private finance would have to be sought to make limited resources go further. A clear strategy on this, it was also thought, would help defuse Tory election tax scares – 'where will the money come from?'[147]

Labour was at that time clear that private finance should not displace the proper role of government. Public responsibilities were not to be transferred to private business. Whatever the mechanisms used – and that was seen as a pragmatic issue – public sector objectives were to remain decisive. Higher returns would obviously have to be paid for private capital. This would need to be justified by the private sector assuming an *appropriate* degree of risk. Private finance was thus simply a means to an end. Contrast this with the Conservatives' Private Finance Initiative where, according to Kenneth Clarke, 'We mean putting the private sector in the driving seat'.[148]

In the early stages of Labour's thinking, the example of pre-privatisation British Airways was influential. It is not generally appreciated that, in the late seventies, only 20 per cent of BA's capital was from public sector sources.[149] The rest was from airline earnings and commercial loans, though the latter were backed by Treasury guarantee. Incidentally, apart from special aid for Concorde, BA then had no subsidy at all. It also had one of the strongest balance sheets of any airline or industry. The lesson was clear. Public objectives could be pursued even where most of the capital wasn't from public sources.

Labour also understood that the case for the Private Finance Initiative was distorted by the Treasury's peculiar definition of the Public Sector Borrowing Requirement (PSBR). According to the PSBR rules, if a public body directly approaches capital markets to fund a project, that counts as public borrowing. On the other hand, if a private firm raises finance from the same sources for exactly the same public project, it doesn't count towards the PSBR. While in opposition, Labour mercilessly ridiculed this absurd dogma which is shared by no other country.[150] The official Organisation for Economic Co-operation and Development definition of Public Sector Borrowing Requirement, later included in the Maastricht Treaty, would not, for example, count a bond issue by NATS or the London Underground towards the PSBR. Why is it so different in Britain? In the immortal words of an ex-senior Whitehall official, Sir Leo Pliatzky: 'The PSBR is a creation of the Treasury's ... and it is what the Treasury *says* it is.'[151]

These Treasury rules have always been interpreted flexibly when politically convenient. For instance, British Petroleum, under public ownership, was always excluded from the PSBR. Pliatzky explains that this 'was because of the self-denying ordinance under which the government had declared that it would not intervene in the management of the company.'[152] He adds that the Conservatives would have behaved likewise if any privatisation had left them with a majority holding. We thus have the intriguing concept of a Flexible Dogma.

Mr. Blair has continued this approach, applying the PSBR rules rigidly in most areas, while relaxing them for projects like UK regional airports, the Post Office and the Channel Tunnel Rail Link. He inherited a confused situation with NATS where the official machine, under the Conservatives, was pressing for full privatisation, while simultaneously trying to hive off various NATS components under the Private Finance Initiative. How was the latter supposed to work?

How Does The Private Finance Initiative Work?

The Conservatives compelled NATS, against its wishes, to let a 'concession' for its North Atlantic and Scottish air traffic control centres. Under the Private Finance Initiative, a private consortium was supposed to raise the finance to pay for design, development and construction of the two centres. In return, that consortium would be paid for making the facilities available to NATS. Under this approach, the chosen supplier would fund the project by borrowing, using the loan to provide buildings, equipment and staff. The supplier would then be expected to carry most of the risks of failure.[153] Note the resemblance to the government's proposals for the London Underground.

NATS had little enthusiasm for this proposal. At a time of rapid technological change, it saw the danger of getting locked into a monopoly private supplier, perhaps for a quarter century. Any changes to the projects, including prices, would have had to be renegotiated. As nearly all major projects in Information Technology are risky, and frequently run into major problems, this would have been quite likely.[154] Given the contractual 'lock-in', the implications for relative bargaining power are obvious.

In such a sensitive situation, a public body needs to be sure that any private sector 'partner' is capable of inspiring its trust over the long term. Under the Private Finance Initiative, it has only one shot at selecting such a partner. Any mistake could thus have disastrous future results because the requirements have to be fully worked out *before* contracts are signed, and there is little scope for subsequent change. In the normal course of events, many technical aspects would be dealt with at a later stage, in discussion with contractors. The rigid PFI framework compels these to be specified in advance as enforceable contracts. Common sense is thus much harder to apply.

In such cases, the public sector has little control over the technologies used. It may not even retain copyright over software. Against this, the private supplier is supposed to receive little or no money until the systems are working. Payment is usually then by instalments. But the private supplier, to repeat, has the immense advantage of being locked into the project for a quarter century, or more. It will ensure prices that compensate for any conceivable hiccups over the coming years. It would be against the interests of its shareholders to do otherwise. So much for the transfer of risk.[155]

Even so, the Conservatives found private business far from enthusiastic about shouldering the risks they were supposed to take over. With all these problems, the Private Finance Initiative turned out to be a prodigiously wasteful and inefficient way of doing things. In fact, there was little progress under the Conservatives. The Treasury remained steadfast in its faith because the costs of PFI are 'off balance sheet', that is not part of the PSBR. The costs of such projects are hidden in the national accounts, because they are funded by instalments out of revenue. If financed as a lump sum, under the bizarre Treasury Rules, they would count towards the PSBR.

The costs of this irrationality were high. While air traffic was growing rapidly, the Private Finance Initiative delayed the projects in question for several years because of the time required to 'compete the concessions'. NATS also risked having different technologies at its English and Scottish Centres, and between its new and old facilities.[156] What would eventually have happened, we may never know, for the projects collapsed. They are now matters for lawyers, and we can say no more.

Ironically, these Private Finance Initiative projects were also a serious impediment to the outright sale of NATS. Where is the logic in a privatised air traffic control having its main centres owned by other private companies? Naturally enough, prospective buyers of NATS couldn't see any. We thus reach a disturbing conclusion: Blair was ready to inflict an artificial, costly and unworkable scheme onto the public sector – but not onto a private firm!

Is A Public/Private Partnership The Best Solution For NATS?

The government has turned NATS into a 'Public/Private Partnership' (PPP). This is a vague, catch-all term that includes PFI, 'contracting out', 'market testing', 'outsourcing', 'joint ventures', 'benchmarking', and other types of collaboration with private interests. In form, however, NATS is now a conventional private firm under UK company law. The government retains 49 per cent of the shares, while private interests hold 46 per cent, and employees 5 per cent. (As new share capital is issued, the government holding may shrink to 25 per cent.)[157]

Does this government shareholding ensure that NATS will continue to behave as a public service? No, because NATS's prime duty has to be to its shareholders. Consistent with this, the private sector will be allowed to 'have a strategic interest in holding more voting rights than the government'. Furthermore, even in protecting its financial investment, the government will 'not prevent the strategic partner from holding operational control.' The government will appoint board members, but will not try to influence commercial operations.[158]

In legal form, NATS is thus a profit driven company. In support of this concept, the government has fought hard, and successfully, to renegotiate the Eurocontrol scheme, under which each country followed common charging principles. The change now allows European Union air traffic operators to 'make and retain profits'[159] and there can be little doubt that the proposed separation of service provision and regulation is designed to facilitate privatisation. At every turn, the government proclaims the superiority of 'the Equity Model'.[160]

Are there other, less objectionable, ways of raising private funds? Yes, it would have been possible to retain a public sector ethos within the Public/Private Partnership framework.[161] Throughout the world, public bodies are raising such private capital by approaching finance markets directly. Not even New Zealand or the USA share Mr. Blair's enthusiasm for privatisation. Available techniques include: (a) non-recourse debt, a type of bond where the greater part of the risk stays with lenders; (b) a Canadian-style not-for-profit Trust with a Board representing government, users, unions and other interests; and (c) an Independent Publicly Owned Corporation (IPOC), a Companies Act model with all shares retained by government. Any of these arrangements could avoid the negative effects of privatisation. They were rejected on ideological grounds.[162]

Can NATS Work As A Commercial Operation?

The trouble is that many vital NATS activities are not at all suited to profit making. Examples are the Distress and Diversion Unit, the Aeronautical Information Service, the Lower Airspace Radar Service, the Meteorological and Information Services. These functions also serve private pilots flying light aircraft. Charging could well 'price them away'. But that doesn't mean that they all would stop flying. They might simply stop using these services. Free market economists would say: 'If they're so stupid, serve 'em right!' Unfortunately, that isn't the point. Private flying often interacts with transport operations, and the latter could be put at risk. Marketisation could thus have a perverse effect.

A commercially driven NATS can hardly be expected to invest in such services as a public duty. Neither can it be expected to take a wide and long term view of airspace development. Many transport investments have long gestation periods, extended economic lives and uncertain outcomes. Think of the railway West Coast Main Line. After many years of travail, this project is still bogged down in confusion.[163] The costs and benefits of such complex schemes are hard to measure. They can often only be justified in social terms, like users' time savings, accident prevention or environmental benefits.

It is natural for a private company to focus on profits instead of bothering about such wider effects. The throughput of any transport facility can always be maximised by having a queue of vehicles waiting to use it. A privatised NATS might thus be tempted to increase throughput by 'stacking' aircraft, instead of trying to reduce the airlines' costs.[164]

The profit imperative works against long-term projects because their returns, in later years, are so heavily 'discounted away'. Demanding a high return also dictates a quick pay back. It is sometimes argued that 'short termist' firms are making some kind of an intellectual mistake. They are doing nothing of the kind. If profit maximisation is the aim, such behaviour is entirely 'rational' from the shareholders' point of view. For the same reason, the requirement for a high commercial return may rule out long term schemes altogether.[165] On this basis, an investment to maintain safety in congested airspace may result in zero, or even negative, returns for a privatised NATS.

The NATS Public Private Partnership thus creates a structural contradiction between public and private objectives, just as with airports and railways. The point is well illustrated by a headline in the technical journal, *Modern Railways*: 'Signalling investment crisis deepens. Railtrack was adamant that investment in signalling doesn't make a business case.'[166] But criticisms of Railtrack on that account were beside the point. That company's prime duty was to its shareholders.

The general public thus had to bear the costs of making Railtrack profitable enough to persuade it to undertake social investments. This has been attempted by raising Railtrack's earnings ('increasing the regulated asset base'), giving them direct public grants, and boosting the subsidies to train operating companies. Note the parallel with London's airports. (As we write, the government is moving to convert Railtrack into a 'Not For Profit' company, but shows no sign of dealing seriously with the deep rooted structural contradictions of the railway industry.)

Then How Does the Government Justify Infrastructure Privatisation?

The government is not eager to discuss such awkward problems. Some insight into its underlying thought processes may be gained from the 'debate' about the London Underground infrastructure. The government claimed that the costs of a Public/Private Partnership for London Transport would be 20-30 per cent lower than with a bond issue – an alleged saving of £4.5 billion. Less prominence was given to the fact that this rested almost wholly on the claim that the Public/Private Partnership could reduce costs in the same way as did Railtrack's infrastructure sub-contractors.[167]

It was assumed that such economies couldn't be made under public ownership. However, British Railways consistently reduced its infrastructure costs over the years, and that trend would have continued. The public sector has great experience of sub-contracting, and doesn't need Public/Private Partnership to secure appropriate economies. Note that word 'appropriate': cost reductions can be pressed much too far. Railtrack and its sub-contractors, which the government take as their model, may well have made that mistake. As far back as 1999, the Railway Regulator pointed out that the track was ageing, its quality worsening and broken rails increasing, while the Health and Safety Executive believed this had the 'potential to erode safety margins'.[168] As Railtrack's technical director has recently conceded, 'The truth is that post privatisation contracting strategy has not worked.'[169] Since these lines were first written, events have tragically confirmed this analysis.

Then a Ministerial allegation that projects led by the public sector always overrun budget in both time and cost. This was especially aimed at London Underground (LU), using a comparison between the Lewisham extension of the Docklands Light Railway and the Jubilee Line. The former was alleged to have been built to time and within budget. On the other hand, the latter massively overran on both counts. In size and complexity, however, these projects had little in common. The Jubilee Line was delayed by signalling and tunnelling problems for which private contractors, not London Underground, were responsible. A more appropriate comparison including the Croydon Tramlink or West Midlands Metro would reveal a quite different story.

What really matters is the quality of management, and naïve assertions that public sector managers are somehow inferior is no more than blatant prejudice. Public sector managers didn't perform badly with Waterloo International station and the hugely complex East Coast Main Line electrification. Compare that with the experience of the Channel Tunnel Link Railway. And what about the costs of the West Coast Main Line project? In the space of a few years, unbelievably, these have almost *quadrupled*. Despite this, the scheme has not yet achieved a timetable acceptable to the Train Operating Companies.[170]

We mention railway infrastructure because that is the Government's favoured comparison, even though it is buried in official 'small print'. But the Public/Private Partnership advocates are strangely reluctant to use their own prime argument. Instead we are told, for instance, that privatisation led to huge staff economies at British Airways.[171] As already pointed out, BA was profitable under public ownership; but it had to shed labour because of the onward march of technology – bigger aircraft, mechanisation of ground functions, and the merger of the former divisions – Overseas, European and Regional.

With the big traffic downturn of the early eighties, the gearing effect described earlier led to major airlines incurring heavy financial losses. Since the mid seventies, BA had worked out a range of slimming exercises, and it was these which were implemented, the aim being to reduce staff numbers to 35,000 by the end of 1983[172]. As any manager knows, such an exercise requires years of planning. It was worked out jointly with the BA trade unions, long before privatisation.

As for the claim that privatisation led to greater efficiency, the best published measure is 'overall break even load factor'. This takes account of both costs and revenues: the more efficient an airline, the smaller the aircraft load required to cover costs. As BA's route structure was relatively stable during the period, with passenger growth and bigger, more cost-effective aircraft, one would expect higher efficiency, despite the long term trend to decreasing unit revenue ('yield dilution').

But the opposite happened. British Airways' break-even load factor increased massively from 55.2 in 1984 to 64.8 in 1991. It still hovers around that level.[173] We could spend much time discussing this result. A BA manager could reasonably argue that the airline's strategy did not aim to reduce costs. It emphasised marketing, and this led to heavy expenditure. This is probably right, but it wholly invalidates the government's argument.

As for comparisons between public and private airlines, a report to the European Commission by US experts said that: (a) 'The overall labour productivity of European flag carriers is low to average. Only three are slightly better than average: Lufthansa, Sabena and Air France.'[174] (All three were publicly owned at the time.) (b) 'British Airways' above average costs were compensated by good yields.'[175] (c) 'There is no clear evidence that airlines which are privately owned or stock-market quoted produce higher returns on equity than state-owned carriers.'[176]

Note that all this relates to more than a decade ago, well before any alleged gains from the threat of privatisation.

All these propositions need to be put in perspective. As already pointed out, British Airways could legitimately argue that its emphasis was on 'branding', that is marketing, and not on cost reduction. But whatever qualifications we make, it is obvious that simplistic claims such as 'private equals efficient' and 'public the opposite' are simply rubbish. So how does 'New' Labour purport to show that PFI/PPP schemes offer 'value for money'?

Are PFI And PPP Schemes 'Value For Money'?

It is impossible to probe the detail of most PFI/PPP schemes. That is because the government invariably says the data is 'commercially confidential'. It also puts much effort into confusing the issues. Part of this is to assert that a public sector 'Comparator' offers an adequate safeguard. This supposedly means that it has to be clearly demonstrated that a private sector solution is superior to one involving the public sector. Otherwise the National Audit Office (NAO) would condemn such schemes as a waste of public money.

But the National Audit Office, like other public bodies, has to work within the framework laid down by the Treasury. An important role here is played by the restrictive Public Sector Borrowing Requirement definition. An even more effective device is the public sector Test Discount Rate (TDR). This sounds like an obscure technical point but the basic idea is straight forward. A test discount rate is no more than a minimum required rate of return on a public investment. (It is called a 'discount' rate because of the way project returns are worked out.) Note that this has nothing to do with the interest which the public sector would actually have to pay on any finance it raises.

In that case, what *does* the Test Discount Rate represent? It is supposed to reflect the return which the *private* sector ought to expect from such a project – currently six per cent in real terms. What has that to do with the public sector? This artificial figure has no significance for the *actual* flows of cash and investment funds. Finance markets might currently provide public sector funding at four or five per cent. We are thus talking about a notional rate of return. Even when hospital trusts repay the Treasury with so-called 'wooden money', they still have to generate that six per cent.[177]

In Mrs. Thatcher's time, the rationale was that public investment might 'crowd out' that of the private sector. More recently, the stress has been on stimulating efficiency, i.e. by forcing public enterprises to secure a high rate of return. Using such an artificially high Test Discount Rate is an effective way of fixing the public sector 'Comparator'. It builds a private sector solution into the calculations. But some of the most eminent specialists favour a 'social discount rate' in the evaluation of public sector projects, that is a much lower figure. Indeed, in a more tolerant political climate, the Treasury was open to such a concept. For the logic is clear. As Professor Lichfield puts it: 'In the short term, how can individual investors reflect changing values in time over the future, particularly when the future must be seen over a long life cycle in natural resources or the built heritage?'[178] He quotes some of the most eminent economists, such as Professor Pigou, who questioned the need for such a discount rate at all.[179]

It is thus clear that the Treasury's choice of Test Discount Rate figure is wholly arbitrary. It has no serious theoretical or practical basis. Its aim is to make public enterprises behave like private firms, and to bias public/private comparisons in favour of the latter.

The Test Discount Rate is another Flexible Dogma. For instance, it does not apply to Scotland. However flimsy the rationale, the effects of using such a high Test Discount Rate are enormous. When public and private schemes are compared for hospitals, London Transport or NATS, the costs of the public options are inflated to an almost comical degree. If a discount rate of, say, five and a half per cent was used instead of six, practically all the PFI/PPP schemes would immediately fall. If the real cost of capital was used, as assessed by private capital markets, privatisation would sink without trace.[180]

But all this discussion is academic from the point of view of the public finances. The plain fact is that just about all British public capital requirements could be met from conventional sources, given the strength of the national fiscal position.[181] Rather than invest in social infrastructure, Messrs. Blair and Brown prefer to pay off the national debt. The government's real motivation, it is clear, is to bring in private capital and management for its own sake. The Treasury justifies this on the basis that private interests will ensure higher efficiency and service quality. How will this work in the case of NATS?

Will Privatisation Lead To Higher Efficiency And Operational Standards?

The primary concern of airspace users is that operational standards should be kept up to a satisfactory level. It would be wrong to suggest that anyone in air transport would ever ask 'how much money can we save if we don't mind killing a few more passengers?' That never happens, but let us pose another question. Where profit maximisation is the major objective, and where there are possible trade offs between costs and operational standards, where will the benefit of the doubt tend to fall?

World experience suggests it will increasingly tend to fall in one direction. An organisation which has always placed overriding weight on safety will *have* to give more emphasis to other objectives. It will not be discouraged from doing so by government policy. This is 'to avoid burdening business with unnecessary regulation'. The effects of commercial pressures and 'business friendly' enforcement can already be seen.

As the immediate users of air traffic services, what pilots say must be taken seriously. The kind of situation that worries them is where, for example, full radar cover at a busy airport is restricted, on commercial grounds, to daytime hours. This may not look unreasonable in good weather. Increasing the night work load of pilots facing bad winter weather at the end of an exhausting duty may be a different story. And despite the limited provision of controlled airspace in certain areas of Britain, there are cases where no advisory services are provided. The latter tell pilots outside controlled airspace about the whereabouts of other aircraft. There may be room for differences of expert opinion about the need for such flying aids, but the fact is they now tend to be provided only where they 'pay'.[182]

Striking evidence on the general erosion of operational standards throughout the industry has been published by the House of Commons Department of the Environment, Transport and the Regions Transport Select Sub Committee.[183] This extends to routine functions that air passengers never think about. From a large number of examples, it mentions deficiencies in navigation charts, training programmes and fire fighting standards. It was even the case that one segment of UK airspace, relating to North Sea helicopters, had been declared 'critically deficient' by the International Pilots' organisation (IFALPA). Little wonder that, in their evidence, the pilots concluded that 'the British regulatory posture tends ... to be too passive and we consider this to be leading to a reduction of standards in the UK aviation industry.'[184]

Can Regulators Deal With The Problems Caused by Privatisation?

This is the climate in which privatisation is being driven further than ever before. The government asserts that regulation will maintain high safety standards. To create an independent safety regulator is the rationale behind separating NATS from the Civil Aviation Authority. It is based upon a complete lack of understanding of the problems. Splitting the functions is supposed to create 'transparency'. Unfortunately, it does the opposite. At the Civil Aviation Authority, the operational head of NATS used to have an office adjacent to the economic and safety regulators. Information was shared between the functional heads. Co-operation was usually smooth. Everybody knew what was going on. Any problems were quickly sorted out. After all, they were colleagues, and had little motive to do anything but work together.[185]

Splitting these functions creates tensions which were not hitherto present. Information becomes harder to get. Facts tend to be dressed up. Regulators can't challenge them without 'peering inside' the undertaking. There is a drift towards statistical, political and legal conflict. This worsens over time. Soon, external regulators can exert only limited influence because -

● To do their job effectively, they need good *co-operation* with those being regulated – very difficult with a basic conflict of objectives.

● They are best at stopping things *after* they have begun – positive action is much more complex and difficult.

● Operational standards involve *judgements* – a series of decisions, each one not too unreasonable in isolation may, in the longer run, add up to a wholesale culture change.

The latter is a gradual process, but it is much influenced by commercial pressures. The process has been superbly analysed by a leading aviation expert, J.M. Ramsden, who calls it 'subtle corporate incapacitation'.[186] The prevailing free market orthodoxy denies any link between financial pressures and operational standards, but this is absolute nonsense. The majority of large scale transport accidents in recent times have shown a clear such link. No wonder the airline pilots call for 'a vigorous approach to enforcement in the public interest.'[187]

Does Airline Ownership Of NATS Solve These Problems?

Such was the opposition to the privatisation of NATS that, for the first ever time, the British airlines agreed on a policy issue. They put forward a 'not-for-commercial-profit' proposal.[188] In the face of such pressure, the government climbed down, and accepted the bid of the airline consortium to take control of NATS.

The compromise forced onto Tony Blair, we can readily accept, is superior to his Equity Model. The airlines will not consciously take risks with operational standards. But this is still, in form, a conventional private company. Under Company Law, it must put shareholders' interests first. It also raises a new set of problems. How will NATS deal with operators outside the airline consortium? How will Civil Aviation Authority regulators adjust the usual Retail Price Index – X formula to reflect the 'not-for-commercial-profit' objectives? (So far, they haven't!) And what if the owners' main airline businesses get into financial difficulties?

The airlines borrowed to pay for NATS' assets, and thus have to pay loan interest. They also need to raise funds for future investments. The public NATS always produced a tidy surplus for the Treasury, but the government had to rescue the privatised company after only a few months.[189] The exercise will almost certainly have to be repeated. (These cash infusions may well be an illegal 'state aid' under European Union legislation.) As for the much vaunted £1 billion in new investment, this was immediately thrown into question.

It was never clear how a privatised NATS could generate enough cash to finance such investments, as well as repay interest, even if maximum profits were not sought. The (starting) regulatory regime demands a cost reduction of five per cent a year. It is hard to see how 'labour efficiencies' can safely produce this. The prospect of long term financial difficulties is thus not merely theoretical. There is an intriguing prospect of NATS becoming insolvent. In that case, would the government allow UK airspace to be closed? Obviously not. But if the Treasury is always going to be the saviour of last resort, what significant risks have been transferred to the private sector?

The government apparently believes that air traffic control, like airports, railways, and the London underground, is not essentially different from dealing in second hand cars or scrap metal. Yet even the Treasury's intellectual hero, Adam Smith, strongly opposed private ownership of infrastructure. In *The Wealth of Nations*, he pointed out that 'The tolls for the maintenance of a high road cannot with any safety be made the property of private persons [because they] might neglect altogether the repair of the road, and yet continue to levy very nearly the same tolls ... At many turnpikes ... the money levied is more than double of what is necessary for executing, in the completest manner, the work which is often executed in a very slovenly manner and sometimes not executed at all.'[190]

We see numerous examples of this profound truth in a modern setting. Adam Smith concluded that transport infrastructure should be managed by 'commissioners or trustees.' He would certainly have taken that same view with air traffic control. For NATS essentially provides a public good, just like a series of lighthouses. These exist for the safety of shipping, with their finance a secondary consideration. They cannot be entrusted to 'private persons'. In Britain, at the height of *laissez-faire*, such lighthouses were taken into a public trust.[191] For harsh experience shows that ownership really *does* matter.

Does Institutional Fragmentation Create A More Effective Industry?

Mr. Blair's 'reforms' go far beyond privatisation. They involve the fragmentation of well-tried institutions. For almost three decades, the Civil Aviation Authority was a classic example of transport integration, which the government claims to support. It was created after the most substantial investigation ever undertaken into British aviation, viz. the Edwards Report.[192] The dismantling of the Civil Aviation Authority did not follow an analysis of similar weight. It has been based on the simplistic dogmas which dominate the policy thinking of Blair's government.

The organisation has been split into NATS, a CAA regulatory body and a joint CAA/RAF body, the Directorate of Airspace Policy. This has added to the bewildering array of bodies with an interest in aviation. But this proliferation shows no sign of leading to better decisions. It flows out of the dogma that there is no higher rationality than that of a profit maximising firm.

Undeterred by its lack of economic success,[193] the British government is still reshaping itself as a tenuously related collection of private firms. These offer, not leadership, but services to customers. There is no co-ordination, no forward thinking, no strategy. As Professor Colin Crouch says, 'The British approach is to make a virtue of the short term logic of the individual firm incapable of strategic action, and to bend public policy in the further extension of that logic, not to counter it.'[194]

None of this makes any economic, financial or operational sense. The calculations purporting to show otherwise could well be extracts from a play of the absurd like N F Simpson's *One Way Pendulum*. One character, it will be recalled, tried to teach his Speak-Your-Weight Machines to sing the Hallelujah Chorus.[195] Tony Blair's Railtrack In The Sky, and his Railtrack Beneath London's Streets, have similar prospects of success.

- *There is no serious economic, financial or operational case for privatising National Air Traffic Services, and the government's belief that 'private is better' has no basis whatever in practical experience.*
- *The case for PFI/PPP solutions is shamelessly rigged with the help of Flexible Dogmas such as arbitrary PSBR rules, an artificially high test discount rate, and an approach to 'risk' transfer which guarantees that private firms will never lose out financially*
- *Under the 'Equity Model', profit and shareholder value have to take priority, with serious implications for operational standards, long term investment and public service.*
- *These problems cannot easily be solved by external regulation, particularly where there is such a profound conflict between public and private objectives.*
- *The dangers have not been wholly overcome by the sale of NATS to an airline consortium with 'not-for-commercial-profit' objectives, for this raises new problems and the government has already been obliged to rescue this Railtrack In The Sky.*
- *The integration of many functions within the Civil Aviation Authority was based upon the comprehensive analysis by the Edwards Committee, whereas Mr. Blair's policy of disintegration appears to have little or no empirical basis.*

Chapter Five

Globalisation: All Power to International 'Market Forces'?

Aviation has been always global. International co-operation made possible a 'seamless' network of interconnecting services. Now the British government has joined the European Union and USA in trying to break up that network. Their aim is world deregulation, marketisation and privatisation. They call it 'liberalisation', 'normalisation' and 'Open Skies'. For who could possibly favour 'deliberalisation', 'abnormalisation' or 'Closed Skies'?

At this stage, the various policy strands we have discussed come together to form a whole. Nevertheless, it is probably most fruitful to consider various aspects in turn. Accordingly, we start with Britain's air services agreement with the USA ('Bermuda II'). Why should 'New' Labour want to discard it? We then look at the concept of 'Open Skies', first in its restricted American sense, and then in terms of a regime under the World Trade Organisation (WTO)[196]. No-one can be certain about how such radical changes would turn out, but we can identify some fundamental issues. These can be highlighted, in turn, from the point of view of air travellers, aviation workers and national economies. Finally, we ask if there is a workable alternative to handing all power to international market forces.

At the outset, we should note a potential source of confusion. In the present transitional state, there are often (at least) two sets of officials dealing with the same matters, from different angles. One set tackles aviation-specific issues; the other deals with generalised 'competition' aspects. The two functions co-exist, somewhat uneasily. This cumbersome split makes it harder to solve problems, and this is exacerbated by the simplistic approach of the competition authorities. Both these sets of influences have an input into UK/US air services relations, and the European Union regime.

What Is The Logic Of Bermuda II?

It is fashionable now to dismiss Bermuda II[197] as 'restrictive'. There are certainly features which could usefully be reviewed. For example, it may be logical to give a central international role to a publicly-owned 'flag carrier' as British Airways' used to be. It is much harder to justify such privileges for one private operator amongst several. Why that particular company, and not other British airlines? Such issues aside, Bermuda II has been, and still is, highly successful. Like all international treaties, it was a compromise, reflecting the bargaining power of the two parties. As circumstances have changed, it has steadily been revised.[198]

Given the power relationship, there was no way that Britain could have forced the USA into a treaty against American interests. For both countries, the driving forces were the heavy financial losses of their operators in the sixties and seventies, and an acceptance that capacity/frequency competition was responsible for those losses. In addition, in the British view, the US airlines enjoyed unfair advantages in competition.

Even when trans-Atlantic traffic was booming, the growth was often 'profitless'. The dynamics were similar to those we saw in the US domestic context. Too much capacity was generated, and airlines would offer exceptionally low fares to 'get bums on seats'. Once airlines are caught up in such rivalry, they have no alternative but to respond. This kind of competitive spiral would, quite often, lead to extra flights being mounted primarily to carry low fare traffic at a hefty financial loss.[199] On both sides of the Atlantic, it was recognised that the problem could only be solved by regulation. The aim was to prevent the excesses of frequency 'swamping' and 'predatory' pricing, at source. To repeat, both the American and British governments accepted that logic. In 1977, they both signed the treaty.

Under both versions of classical regulation, TransAtlantic fares have come down dramatically over the last thirty years, as Figure Six shows.[200] The previous regime ('Bermuda I') was also very successful, in terms of fares. But the current regime has continued the downward trend, while also producing financial stability for the airlines. (The slight increases of the seventies and eighties were due to fuel crises.). Similarly, traffic has grown, as has the number of airports ('Gateways') served.[201] The long term trend is unmistakable. By any standards, this is a highly successful regime.

Until recently, however, the two governments took different views on the rules of the competitive game. The vast networks of the US

MegaCarriers are closed to non-American airlines. The US carriers thus control the lion's share of international 'feed' traffic into their fortress hub/gateways. They can set fares on those feeder routes to maximise their overall profitability between the American interior and the ultimate foreign destination. It may even pay them to subsidise the US domestic segment, in order to control that traffic. This explains the strange anomalies where it may cost less to fly from London to, say, a point in Arizona, changing planes at Atlanta, than it would to end the journey in Atlanta itself. Experienced travellers book the through ticket, and throw away the domestic coupon.[202] British operators have no such 'behind' feeder routes in the USA. They must persuade other US airlines to carry their traffic to and from the interior of America. The US MegaCarriers thus have a substantial built-in advantage.

On the European shores, reflecting their post war ascendancy, the Americans had many traffic rights between Britain and other countries. PanAm even had a fleet based in London which fed traffic into its trans-Atlantic services. US airlines, on both sides of the Atlantic, thus started with a base traffic which was not available to their foreign rivals. It gave them a head start in frequency competition. A lone British operator, facing two such US airlines thus had an unequal struggle.

Under Bermuda II, to counter this imbalance, each country has broadly the same number of routes. A single British airline now tends to face only one American rival. Above a certain traffic volume, there may be two carriers from each side. But a capacity pre-screening mechanism damps down the wastes of scheduling competition. Tariff regulation keeps uneconomic fares within bounds, while ensuring that travellers are not exploited. Most remarkable of all, the UK authorities can intervene on *internal* US feeder routes to reject predatory tariffs. This approach has been very successful. Bermuda II has allowed British airlines to raise the UK traffic share from a third to almost a half.

Why Dismantle A Successful Regime?

As we noted, the US MegaCarriers don't have an easy life. Some experts believe the American domestic markets to be 'fully mature', in that there is little scope for further growth of business traffic. With so much excess capacity slopping around, international expansion is an attractive prospect. It would be even more so if the US airlines could break free of regulation, win greater access to Heathrow, and fly beyond London wherever they choose.

The USA therefore wants to scrap the Bermuda II designation, capacity and tariff provisions. This American version of 'Open Skies' demands unlimited feeder services for its own carriers, at both US and UK Gateways.[203] This is illustrated in Figure Seven. But the USA will not allow foreign operators onto its domestic routes, or allow them to take over American airlines. Neither will it scrap discriminatory rules compelling its officials and mails to 'Fly American'. The United States thus retains a protected home base from which its airlines can expand abroad. Many countries have agreed to this asymmetric scheme which is illustrated in Figure Eight.[204] In return, they have been granted more access to the USA, i.e. more Gateways. But the present British carriers already have the Gateways they need, as the treaty has gradually been amended. So many more cities now have TransAtlantic routes. And additional airlines have been able to open services. So why entertain the American demands?

The USA has seized an opportunity offered by the latest phase of airline concentration. American Airlines (the Dallas based operator, AMR), British Airways and others have formed the 'One World' Alliance. (British Midland are linked to Lufthansa and United Airlines in the rival 'Star' Alliance.) These alliances fall short of mergers[205] which are prevented by the nationality clauses in air services agreements. Nevertheless the Americans claim that the Alliances *must* conform to their Anti-trust and Competition Laws. They accordingly refuse to approve those Alliances unless Britain agrees to the US interpretation of Open Skies.

This kind of power game is not new. The Americans frequently try to impose their laws on the rest of the world. In their opinion, it is even illegal for the British *authorities* to call their airlines together to discuss UK/US fares. At one time, British governments stoutly resisted these extraterritorial claims. In recent times, they have allowed disputes between UK airlines to be settled in the US courts.[206] Nowadays, the UK government apparently feels that American judges can make better decisions on disputes between British airlines than its own regulators.

Figure Six U.K. / U.S. Air Fares in Perspective
Real Transatlantic Yields Have Declined by Two-Thirds in the Last 30 Years

Yield per Revenue Passenger Mile (1995)

1964 1966 1968 1970 1972 1974 1976 1978 1980 1982 1984 1986 1988 1990 1992 1994

Year   Yield = average fare per passenger mile in
        U.S. $ (constant 1995 prices)

Source: Roberts, Roach and Associates Inc.

These legal mechanisms are quite distinct from the air services agreements. The treaties hardly mention them. For the USA claims that its own legal processes cannot be bound by international agreements.[207] So there is an ever-present danger that some US Anti-trust law or decision will be activated so as to nullify an agreement like Bermuda II. Such an action could even be brought by a private interest.

For many years, it was British policy to make counter demands, including the 'opening' up of the internal US market to foreign airlines, abolishing discriminatory practices like 'Fly American' and retaining some regulatory overview. But the American response is invariably 'that's our model; take it or leave it!' Those British airlines which are in an Alliance with US carriers now tend to accept the American position, while those frozen out are bitterly opposed. The former are no doubt influenced by the promise of access to the vast US domestic networks of their Alliance partners. But what do the rest of us gain from these Alliances?

The Alliance protagonists stress such alleged benefits as lower fares, wider choice of destinations and 'seamless' connections. But the classical IATA system provided all that. Under deregulation, airlines often refuse to connect with other carriers. Remarkably, even the European Commission is now dimly beginning to perceive some of these realities.[208] These are made clear in the industry's own marketing textbook. The Alliance members will strive to halt the continual erosion of passenger fares and freight rates. They hope to control their high yield traffic, as explained earlier, by emphasising 'branding'. With this goes code sharing, blocked space arrangements, 'funnel flights' and even revenue pooling.[209] In the name of lofty principle, the real aim is to get back some of the certainties of the old bilateral regimes. For the airlines, this makes perfect sense. But there will be no effective mechanisms to protect users. In effect, this is the ultimate privatisation – that of regulation itself.

This is the context in which the Americans offer Anti-trust immunity to the Alliances in return for scrapping Bermuda II. Two British airlines[210] would no doubt gain short term advantages from doing so. But long term, and probably irreversible, changes would be conceded in the regulatory regime. Over the past few decades, British

Airways has had commercial ties with American, United and US Airways. All have failed. Can we have any more confidence that the present AA/BA Alliance will last? But once Bermuda II has gone, it will be almost impossible to get it back.

But how could American operators fly unlimited services into the Heathrow or Gatwick when there are no spare slots for them? The answer is ... full blooded *marketisation*. American carriers want to buy whatever London slots they need.[211] Those slots would almost certainly be purchased from small British carriers on short haul services. The demand for the slots would be high because the Americans already have traffic rights to fly between just about any pair of European Union countries. While enjoying those rights, continental America would remain tightly shut against any airline not in Alliance with a US carrier.

Could The European Union As A Bloc Counter American Power?
At this point, the European Commission argues that, if the EU negotiated as a bloc, it could force the USA to accept a more balanced regime.[212] Any American carrier can already operate between almost any pair of EU airports, because of the Open Skies agreements it has with individual member countries. Moreover, there is no control on the US airlines' frequency or capacity, and virtually none over its fares. Now that the European Commission appears to have won 'external competence'[213], why not even things up by facing the Americans as a unified EU bloc?

From a European view, there is much to be said for the EU using its power in this way. Unfortunately, however, the European Commission doesn't view this as an opportunity to negotiate an EU/US *managed* regime, on the lines of Bermuda II. It wants to see a great extension of market forces, in the form of a Trans Atlantic Competition Area. Its bargaining power would be confined to pressing for 'a level playing field'. Its vision is one of Air France, Alitalia or Lufthansa operating to the USA from London, while British Airways, British Midland and Virgin do the same from Paris, Rome or Frankfurt. This presupposes an end to US discriminatory practices and a common EU/US Competition Law. This regime would thus project US deregulation onto an international scale.[214]

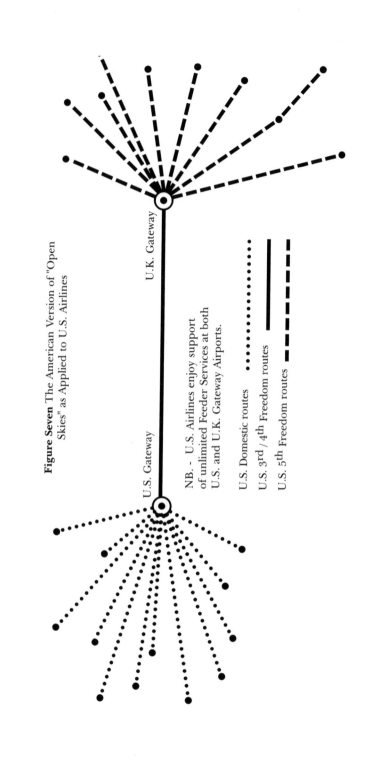

Figure Seven The American Version of "Open Skies" as Applied to U.S. Airlines

U.S. Gateway

U.K. Gateway

NB. - U.S. Airlines enjoy support of unlimited Feeder Services at both U.S. and U.K. Gateway Airports.

••••••••• U.S. Domestic routes

───────── U.S. 3rd / 4th Freedom routes

▬ ▬ ▬ ▬ U.S. 5th Freedom routes

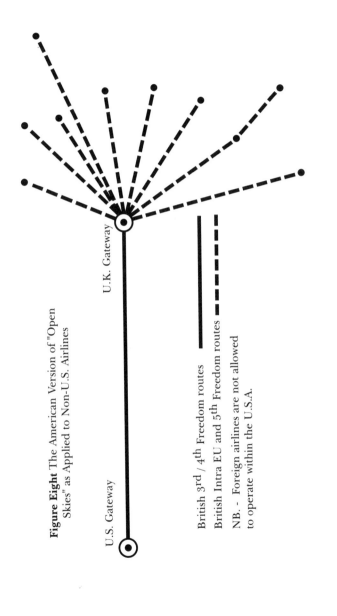

Figure Eight The American Version of "Open Skies" as Applied to Non-U.S. Airlines

U.S. Gateway

U.K. Gateway

British 3rd / 4th Freedom routes

British Intra EU and 5th Freedom routes

NB. - Foreign airlines are not allowed to operate within the U.S.A.

Naturally, the British want to go much further. The Civil Aviation Authority suggests including aviation within the General Agreement on Trade in Services (GATS). 'Open Skies', claims the CAA, is an idea to which 'every right thinking person can lend their support'.[215] But the Authority is also well aware that most countries rarely in practice show 'a selfless devotion to the ideals of free trade.' It accordingly urges scrapping 'all existing constraints' on routes, frequencies, and tariffs, plus the ending of ownership and control restrictions. This would permit 'unrestricted access' by foreign airlines to all countries' domestic as well as international markets. The World Trade Organisation (WTO), 'with its emphasis on eliminating barriers to entry in the market' is the ideal framework, 'leaving airlines much freer to pursue their commercial interests', subject only to general Competition Law.[216]

This is wholesale deregulation on a truly world scale. Nowhere do its protagonists even try to offer any evidence or argument to justify such a radical course. It is all based on *a priori* reasoning. So let us ask how Open Skies may affect the interests of travellers, employees and wider national economies.

How Can 'Open Skies' Benefit Travellers?

There is no reason to suppose that world deregulation would be any better for air travellers than it has been within the USA. Open Skies would quickly become the preserve of a handful of MegaCarriers, based on existing Alliances and Computerised Reservations Systems. There would no doubt be many more operators, but they would be limited to regional, specialised or niche markets. The airlines are all too aware that competition generates excess capacity. They would be at pains to avoid 'commoditisation' – where airline tickets are part of a spot market like those for grain or cotton futures. They would 'segment' their markets, brand their 'products', and extract the highest possible fares from each group of 'customers'. The existing Alliance systems are designed for the same purpose as the US hub and spoke networks. Just about all the benefits claimed for them could be enjoyed under the traditional bilateral system.[217] But consumers would effectively lose what regulatory protection they now enjoy.

Just what the government has in mind in the way of user protection has been revealed in an obscure administrative change. This has already come in where deregulation has taken place. Within the UK domestic and EU regimes, the CAA has abolished its 'Tariff Filing' system.[218] This was a mechanism for rendering tariffs intelligible, where they would otherwise be confusing, contradictory and sometimes incomprehensible. Without such a system, there can be no meaningful scrutiny of fares and their conditions. For the CAA will not even know what the fares are. Only 'whistle blowing' airlines will thus be in a position to make informed complaints. The government could hardly signal more clearly that deregulation should work for airlines, and not the travelling public.

But we are forgetting the role of competition in protecting air users. No doubt, the World Trade Organisation could supervise a truly global regime based on that principle. How might this work? Free market economists strongly believe in Flags of Convenience, so they can hardly complain if we look for precedents in shipping.[219]

The International Maritime Organisation (IMO) would be the obvious model for any WTO regime. But the European Commission itself has denounced IMO as 'toothless' and 'irrelevant'. In return for cash, according to the Commission's Head of Maritime Safety, ship owners can buy a hassle free address from Flag of Convenience nations.[220] The trade organisation of tanker owners recently accused one such country, with more than twenty per cent of the world fleet, of *never* having investigated a sea accident. This is in the context of 220 (sic) losses of ships in the last five years.[221]

At the same time, the UK's Chief Marine Accident Investigator has warned that safety standards are falling because of the lengths some shippers will go to make a profit. He is clear that commercial pressures have been a factor in a number of accidents.[222] There is also a relentless decline in the standard of seafaring, and workers are reluctant to speak out for fear of losing their jobs. No doubt it will be argued that aviation starts with immeasurably superior standards, and that is of course true. But the point is how to prevent those standards being driven down.

So world experience offers clear guidance on possible results of these policies-

● The projection of deregulation onto a world scale will have the same results as in the USA, including the generation of surplus capacity and financial instability.

● MegaCarriers will try to maximise their control over passenger traffic flows, using the methods now familiar in America.

● Airlines will charge whatever the market will bear, evolve a mystifying array of tariffs and discriminate between countries and groups of passengers.

● Given the problems of applying Competition Law, MegaCarriers will severely discipline low fare 'new entrants' if these become a threat.

● Policy makers will probably counter these problems by encouraging Flags of Convenience but, as shipping demonstrates, this could drag operational standards down to unacceptable levels.

● Consumer groups will have as little influence over the MegaCarriers as motorists over the retail petrol prices of the multinational oil companies.

The greater the intensity of unregulated competition, the more the airlines will be driven, not only to exploit travellers, but also to force down their labour costs. Open Skies therefore also has serious implications for workers in the industry

How Will Open Skies Affect Air Transport Workers?

In air transport, as in other sectors, corrosive forces have been held in check by public ownership, bilateral regulation, nationality of ownership controls, and various other 'market distortions'. Under Open Skies, airlines will be able to shift their operations, slots, work locations, headquarters and ownership to wherever they wish, and in whatever way suits their shareholders. The intensification of competition will shift bargaining power in favour of employers. The latter can adapt to new circumstances, but the profit imperative will allow no let up in the pressure on employees.

How could trade unions respond if some international body declared that there were not enough competitors between London and New York? Suppose a British airline was *compelled* to sacrifice routes, and lay off employees, because room had to be found for other airlines, including foreign operators? This is a real possibility, given existing airport capacity shortages. But there would be little point in trade unions trying to negotiate with the airlines involved because there would be nothing the latter could do about the situation. Employers could legitimately claim *force majeure*. In that situation, a national government could not easily intervene. That would probably also even be true of the European Commission.

Whatever form developments eventually take, it is thus clear beyond doubt that they may have a profound effect upon the bargaining power of trade unions. Flags of Convenience could be used to squeeze down labour costs. The implementation of only a part of this agenda could lead to a decisive shift in power from national regulators to multinational airlines. In these circumstances, there would be little point in lobbying national governments.

Employers tend to argue that, if they can gain 'freedom' from outside intervention, then this is in the interests of their workers. That is because it will allow firms to expand without regulatory hindrance. But once the birds have flown the national regulatory nest, trade unions may find themselves in a very different situation. If an airline's headquarters are outside the unions' own political jurisdiction, it is much more difficult to exert effective pressure on the company, or on the relevant authorities. If, for example, British Airways were to merge with American Airways, given the current structure – with probably more than forty per cent of BA already held by foreign interests – the result would be a US owned company. No doubt, its headquarters would be in Dallas.

European trade unions may thus come under pressure from forces over which they can exert little or no control.

● It would become more difficult legitimately to resist cuts in pay/conditions: 'we have no option because that's the state of the international market!'

● It would become much easier to substitute workers, or even entire flying operations, from low-wage areas for those currently based in EU countries.

● Route structures, and the use of associated carriers, could be manipulated for cost-cutting and anti-union purposes.

● Conversion of airline Alliances into full mergers could lead to (currently European) MegaCarriers being controlled from the USA, and basing their company headquarters there.

● Given a full blooded Competition Law, the governing authorities could rule that certain labour protective mechanisms are 'market distorting'.

● Industrial disputes could be manoeuvred into the law courts of the countries with the most repressive legislation, e.g. the UK, where 'secondary actions' are illegal.

But the implications go much wider. Individual countries' freedom of action to protect their national interests may be radically cut down, or even eliminated. Consider some possibilities.

How Will Open Skies Affect National Economies?

Suppose a major British airline decided to shift its main base/headquarters/hub out of the UK in the interests of its shareholders. Such a shift could take place if aviation were included in the General Agreement on Trade in Services (GATS). (The latter is but one of 28 WTO free trade agreements.) A key feature of GATS/WTO is that enforcement is taken out of the hands of nation states. It is the task of disputes panels, whose conclusions are binding. Sanctions may be taken against states which refuse to abide by their decisions. How would this work in aviation?

The North American Free Trade Agreement (NAFTA) offers an important clue because the USA considers it a model for the world economy. NAFTA embodies the legal theory of 'takings' which holds that public regulation of any kind 'takes' away private property.[223] Property owners are entitled to compensation if private land is taken for a road. On that analogy, there should also be 'fair compensation' in return for regulatory burdens. (The proposed Multinational Agreement on Investment (MAI), which Tony Blair supported, was designed to spread such investors' rights throughout the world. As with NAFTA, disputes panels under MAI would have been able to override national governments.)

That this is far from academic is illustrated by certain cases under NAFTA. Canada banned certain petrol additives because they were held to be polluting water supplies. The US company responsible argued before a tribunal that the ban infringed NAFTA rules. The Canadian government then repealed the ban, paid compensation for lost profits, and discovered it was wrong about the public health danger.[224] Mexico banned a waste disposal project because it believed water supplies were being put at risk. The US company concerned managed to overturn the decision. The plant is now being built in a stream bed.[225] Another case relates to California, but it is hard to say what is happening because, under the rules, consumer bodies, and even governments like California State, are locked out. But it looks as if a facility which California would ban on environmental grounds will go ahead by courtesy of NAFTA.[226]

The action of United Parcels (UPS) against the Canadian government shows how far this process can go.[227] The Canadian post office has a courier business, and UPS claim that this affects its own profitability. No matter that Canada Post is financially self-sufficient; UPS allege that the post office is cross-subsidising its courier business. That is because users can deposit courier mail in letter boxes, and have their packages sorted with the rest of the mail. Almost any aspect of a postal operation could be challenged on such grounds.

It is hardly controversial to suggest that NAFTA and MAI perfectly suit the interests of multinational companies. These initiatives are part of a grand design in which public sector activities throughout the world are being 'opened up' to profit-driven firms. This has special attractions in air transport. At one stroke, the bilateral agreements by which less powerful countries win a reasonable share of their aviation markets would be swept away. Reciprocity would be scrapped. Market forces would reign supreme.

Ironically enough, the chief hesitations come from the Americans. A majority of the Supreme Court justices are now believed to subscribe to the 'Takings' view,[228] but the Bush administration is somewhat ambiguous about a full blooded global free market. If all power is given to the World Trade Organisation, the USA will also have to comply with disputes panel decisions. Already we have seen moves to exempt certain American interests like agriculture, textiles and steel. The Americans would thus clearly prefer arrangements, as with their version of Open Skies, that retain a good deal of protectionism – for themselves.

While no one can predict the impact on individual countries if aviation was included within GATS, we can suggest some serious possibilities –

- Airport access would be on a strictly free market basis, with no more Grandfather Rights, and reserving London slots for, e.g., UK regional services would be illegal.
- Airport expansion would become a purely commercial matter without regard to other concerns such as local authority planning and environmental limits.
- Operators of short distance air services could sue the British government for subsidising 'unfair' competition in the form of inter-city railways.
- Airports could be taken over by foreign interests which would be free to strip assets, shift the main operation to another country, and develop a theme park instead.
- The same could happen to air traffic control systems where capacity would only be installed if profitable, with main centres possibly based abroad and national governments left helpless to intervene in the public interest.
- If America started a trade war with, say, Brazil, China or Russia, it could order US owned airlines, airports or air traffic companies in Europe to halt services to such countries, regardless of the views of national host governments.

None of this, we must stress, is far out. President Bush already has congressional approval for 'fast track' WTO negotiations. The US multinationals are pressing hard for increased access to foreign markets, plus more privatisation and 'liberalisation' of ownership. As in NAFTA, they want WTO Tribunals to override any nation's laws that 'restrain' trade. At the recent Doha negotiation, the Americans brushed aside concerns about human rights, labour standards and environmental protection.[229]

It is an insistent 'New' Labour theme that Britain has no alternative but to embrace global market forces.[230] What is conspicuously missing is any explanation of *why* this should have to be, and why Tony Blair believes that no alternative course possible.

Is There A Workable Alternative To 'Market Forces'?
Whether Britain signs up to the American version of Open Skies, the European Commission's Trans Atlantic Competition Area or the Civil

Aviation Authority's GATS/WTO proposal, it isn't easy to see how travellers, employees and national economies will gain. They may lose a great deal when the global MegaCarriers are 'freed' from nearly all democratic control. If there is still some form of intervention, it will be undertaken by bureaucrats, meeting in camera, with governments probably locked out. It will be aimed solely at facilitating business interests. Experience so far, as with the North American Free Trade Area, allows little scope for any other interpretation.

But 'New' Labour shows no sign of interest in trying to control, or at least moderate, the effects of global 'market' forces. The main thrust of Tony Blair's economic policy is to dismantle regulation of all kinds, particularly in continental Europe. But this is a bizarre misjudgement. The British economy has now been subjected to two decades of such treatment. What improvements have been brought about in the key areas of investment and productivity? If national regulation really has become obsolete, the key task should be how to recapture public governance of the private economy at some relevant international level. As Crouch and Streeck put it, 'Domestic democratic sovereignty over the economy, the only sovereignty that really counts, can be restored only if it is internationally shared.'[231] In aviation, that means an international regime that is managed, and subject to democratic control.

Is international regulation feasible? Free market economists believe that regulators can't rationally decide how many airlines to allow on a route, choose which ones should fly or judge whether their tariffs are right. But classical regulators did this all the time, and successfully. What is more, governments are still doing it. For example, the Americans have a systematic method for carrier selection. They often have to choose which airline should take up a limited international opportunity. The UK hearings system allows rival airlines to battle for route licences in front of an expert panel. Wider issues like network effects, international factors and environmental problems can be brought into the analysis. Even the European Commission admits[232] that it couldn't avoid the issue. In exercising its 'competence' over services between EU countries and non-member states, it would have to make *judgements* about airlines, and thus often also between national interests.

At first glance, the global regulation of fares looks much more difficult. After all, there are millions, perhaps billions, of them. But this again is readily managed. The industry professionals who set up the Civil Aviation Authority's tariff evaluation system worked on a highly selective basis.[233] Under the CAA's approach, airlines proposed their own tariffs. The great majority were 'rubber stamped'. All the Authority did was ensure that any group of passengers was charged a price reasonably related to the costs of providing their seats. 'Captive' passengers were thus protected from being exploited. 'Predatory' fares were stopped at source. Moreover, the costs in question were not always the operator's own costs. The benchmark was an 'efficient' airline. Thus it was possible, if thought necessary, to exert pressure on certain operators. This approach played a significant role helping British Airways to become more efficient. The Conservatives stopped all that because it interfered with privatisation.

The process was further streamlined by highlighting certain 'key' routes. These were investigated in depth, in partnership with the British airlines. And then, within those routes, only 'key' fares were evaluated, for example the 'normal economy' tariff. That approach meant that a surprisingly small number of strategic decisions could shape the entire tariff structure. The technical problems were thus solved long ago.[234] This approach could easily be applied at a European Union level. In fact, the nucleus for doing it already exists in Brussels. The problems are not technical, but entirely political and ideological.

World experience confirms that regulation is best performed by a specialist body, like the classical UK Civil Aviation Authority or the former US Civil Aeronautics Board. 'Generalist' competition regulators, their minds stuffed with ideological mumbo jumbo, have no grounding in aviation technicalities. They cannot deal realistically with issues such as alleged computer hacking, like those in the famous 'Dirty Tricks' controversy between British Airways and Virgin Atlantic.[235]

But doesn't such a managed regime create the spectre of a vast new 'bureaucracy'? As we saw with airport slots, it is the dogmatic pursuit of markets that creates bureaucracy. What could be more bureaucratic than the present situation where a proliferation of bodies are sticking their fingers into the aviation pie? At one time, there was only the Civil Aviation Authority and the Ministry of Transport. Now there is also the Department of Trade and Industry, the Cabinet Office, the Office of Fair Trading, the Competition Commission, the European Commission Transport Directorate (DGIV), the EU Competition Directorate (DGVII), with law courts here, there and everywhere breathing over their shoulders.[236] And we mustn't forget the various US agencies and whatever new 'competition' bodies are on the horizon.

All these agencies work on the utterly false assumption that air transport can function as a self-balancing free market. But aviation is a complex mixture of competition, monopoly and power politics. As John Prescott once explained: 'The market and competition have their role to play. But left to themselves, they are incapable of achieving the necessary objectives of the community. The way forward is one of balance between the market and regulation. The exclusive reliance on competition and markets can be damaging to the national interest.'[237] On this view, policy makers should begin by defining objectives. 'Competition' is not a substitute for those objectives. It may sometimes be a useful mechanism for achieving them. But it is not an end in itself.[238] There are often much better mechanisms for achieving the community's objectives.

As for those objectives, it is hard to share Tony Blair's blind faith in international market forces. What is entirely missing is a cold analysis of the strength of those forces, and the limits within which national governments still have significant room for manoeuvre. To quote John Prescott again, this is 'symptomatic of an intellectual laziness that we cannot afford.'[239] Thinking is hard work, but that is no excuse for 'New' Labour not to make the effort.

- *Bermuda II's success shows how a managed regime can help secure lower fares, wider user choice, financial stability and fair shares of benefits between national interests.*
- *The various forms of Open Skies are no more than the global projection of American deregulation which has had such negative results for airlines, employees and travellers.*
- *The advantages of the new airline Alliances are somewhat exaggerated and*

nearly all their alleged benefits, plus much more, could be secured under managed regimes.

- *Open Skies will involve unrestrained buying and selling of airlines, airports and air traffic services for short term profit and, with power vested in the Visible Hand of multinational companies, will amount to the privatisation of regulation.*
- *There are significant political implications in that such a course would place Britain, and Europe, increasingly under the political power of the USA.*
- *These developments are not inevitable and a streamlined, yet highly effective, international regime could be developed, beginning at EU level, working not just in the interests of shareholders but also of consumers, employees, and the broader community.*

Chapter Six

'Modernisation': Is 'New' Labour's Philosophy Really Modern?

In order to do justice to Tony Blair's aviation policies, we have looked at some specific issues in depth. For the most part, we concluded that 'New' Labour's policies do not flow from any realistic analysis of economic processes. Instead, they appear to be *deduced* from certain *a priori* notions which are apparently assumed to be self-evidently true. Before making definitive judgements, however, we ought to check that we have properly understood the broad thrust of 'New' Labour's thinking. Perhaps Tony Blair has some cosmic arguments for 'modernisation', so powerful that they will brush aside our own analyses as mere technical quibbles.

'Modernisation' is hardly an exact term, so we need criteria with which to test whether any given policy is satisfactorily 'modern'. A useful starting point is Mr Blair's dictum that 'what matters is what works'. We interpret this to mean that truly modern policies must be based upon, or at least consistent with, relevant practices that global experience has shown to be more successful than those followed in Britain until now. Such criteria may be summed up as Relevance, Workability and Superiority.

About half a dozen prominent strands in Tony Blair's general thinking have significant policy implications for aviation. As the industry is still so much influenced by governmental decisions, it is logical to begin with 'New' Labour's political strategy. We next consider the scientific authority of the doctrines that broadly guide, or are used to justify, Blair's economic policies. Then we enquire into the relevance of such themes as the 'New' Economy, 'labour market flexibility' and the crucial role of small firms. Finally, we gauge the extent to which 'New' Labour is in touch with the world's most advanced industrial practices.

Will Political Modernisation Help Ensure A Better Future For Aviation?

The obvious place to look for clues on 'New' Labour's political strategy is in Mr. Blair's speeches. These are replete with terms like 'new', 'reform', 'service delivery', 'targeting', 'best value', 'dynamic

91

market economy', 'end of boom and bust', 'joined up thinking', 'we must all work together', 'core values', 'ending social exclusion', 'no more tax and spend', 'standing up to the enemies of change', 'true Britishness', 'tough decisions', 'traditional values in a modern setting', 'crackdown', 'modernisation', etc. etc. etc.

Unfortunately, it is hard to extract any operational meaning[240] from this. In his authoritative *Critique of Pure Verbiage*, Ronald Englefield characterises such language as verbal reflexes which are 'vaguely associated with certain general emotional situations but are not linked to any clear idea'.[241] Of course, such reflexes often serve a definite political, literary or religious purpose. But looking for policy substance in a Blair speech is rather like expecting to find advice on foot and mouth disease in Beethoven's *Pastorale*.

Perhaps the most informative source on 'New' Labour's political strategy is the work of Dick Morris who masterminded Bill Clinton's 1996 re-election campaign.[242] Though unquestionably original, Morris's words have an uncannily familiar ring. He even appears to have invented the tactic of winning parents' votes by attacking school teachers, back in Clinton's time as an Arkansas politician.[243] One of Morris's most influential ideas is that of 'Triangulation'. This aims to blend 'the best' of rival 'left' and 'right' wing parties' views, while also 'transcending' them.[244] In British terms, that means meeting the needs of Conservative 'swing' voters in a way that is distinctively 'New' Labour.

On this view, policies should be aimed at 'functional' groups, defined with the help of opinion surveys.[245] One such group, for example, may be young professional couples who are anxious to get ahead, secure a bigger mortgage and do the best for their children. Tax cuts will be popular with them, and these should be precisely targeted. A 'left wing' party can neutralise political opposition by 'fast forwarding' the right wing agenda. That means slashing public spending, 'reforming' welfare, acting tough on crime, downsizing government, and cutting down on regulation. For obvious reasons, this will rob Conservatives of much of their appeal.[246]

Morris is firm that, to 'retain a permanent majority', a government must campaign every single day. The cardinal rule is: 'if sixty per cent of voters favour something, we support it too!' Most of this 'new' policy agenda consists of 'small bricks': improving people's lives in small, but specific, ways. That doesn't rule out occasional controversy, because people value Big Leadership. But leaders should *never* give any impression of changing their minds.[247] This is particularly true of foreign policy which plays a key role in telling voters about the personalities of their leaders. Using force abroad can wipe out any image of weakness and vacillation, in favour of resolution and toughness. In this context, Morris is reported as saying 'Yeah, well, they're slaughtering the Bosnians but so what? I want to bomb the shit out of the Serbians to make the President look strong.'[248]

In its own terms, Morris's approach clearly *is* 'modern', and has had a profound influence on 'New' Labour. It helps to explain, for example, why Blair persists with Conservative 'free market' notions, refuses to drop flawed policies like NATS privatisation, and engages in so much meaningless 'targetry'. However, Morris's prime expertise is in winning elections, not advising on 'Nine Till Five' politics. It is here that corridor pressures and vested interests come into play. It is the job of civil servants to weigh up the relative forces, and make policy recommendations. In doing so, the officials concerned would strongly reject any charge of bias. But all policy ideas rest on assumptions, even if only implicit. For their part, pressure groups are rarely able to suggest any coherent policies that transcend their immediate demands. This is particularly true of the business people who staff the huge network of Task Forces. As Blair's own advisers ('policy wonks') work at a highly subjective level, this often leaves an operational vacuum. No matter: the official economists stand ready to fill it. In Whitehall, simplistic free market theories enjoy a status almost akin to the science used to design aeroplanes.

Are 'New' Labour's Economic Theories Self-Evidently True?

In official pronouncements, the free market dogmas are *asserted*, and not argued out. For a long time, they have simply been taken for granted. In the 1960s, for example, Harold Wilson deregulated road haulage, stripped the railways of their road 'feeder' vehicles and freight marketing capability and carried out Dr Beeching's system cuts.[249] Labour did this while believing it was pursuing transport 'Integration'.[250] As each new Minister arrives, Whitehall dusts off its favourite policies, and submits them afresh. Perhaps the best example is the sustained campaign, dating from the early 1960s, to bring in electronic road pricing.[251] Traffic engineering offers a much better solution to road congestion.[252] But road pricing has irresistible attractions because it is seen as a big step towards 'markets' in roads. Such ideas have won a new lease of life because 'New' Labour rhetoric 'unshackles' free market economists from any bounds of reality.

Although often wrapped up in off-putting mathematics, these notions are no more than a simplistic version of the economic orthodoxy which grew out of Adam Smith's famous Invisible Hand. There are various sub-schools, such as 'monetarism', 'rational expectations' and 'supply side economics', but all are based on the core belief that, if every individual behaves selfishly in a perfectly free market, their competitive interactions will ensure the greatest possible happiness for all.[253] This is the core of what is supposed to be a 'clear, unequivocal, unsullied, and empirically verified' theory'.[254]

And yet, there is controversy in the higher reaches of economics of a kind not found in physics, engineering or aircraft design. As Professor Steve Keen points out: 'for over a century, *economists* have shown that economic theory is replete with logical inconsistencies, specious assumptions, errant notions, and deductions contrary to empirical data.'[255] [Emphasis added.] The fact is that the ruling orthodoxy is riddled with *internal* contradictions. No-one has ever been able to *prove* that the Invisible Hand works for the general benefit of Humankind.[256]

Surely, if this were true, the intellectual weaknesses of free market economics would quickly be exposed? Unfortunately, it doesn't work like that. As Professor Alfred Eichner explains: 'Criticisms are rejected, not because they lack intellectual merit, but, rather because they go against the grain of the prevailing orthodoxy. No appeal to the evidence will succeed. Only the evidence which accords with *a priori* belief is acknowledged. Economics has, in this respect, become a closed system of ideas, more like a religion than a science.'[257]

Eichner's view is supported in perhaps the most learned contribution to this subject in recent times. Professor Homa Katouzian highlights the rising trend for neo-classical theorists to propose ideas which are not empirically testable. He believes that the 'ancient preoccupation' ... [with] 'the existence and stability of general equilibrium systems' [i.e. free markets] ... is more dominant than at any time in the past.'[258] Katouzian thinks that the main influence is the use of mathematics in an attempt to achieve high scientific status. The real game is solving puzzles, not studying real economies. In other words, the prevailing theory is not being tested against real life but is becoming increasingly remote from it.[259]

These views are broadly shared by some of the world's most famous economists. For example, Harvard Professor and Nobel Prize Winner, Wassily Leontiev, has asked: 'How long will researchers working in adjoining fields, such as demography, sociology, and political science ... and ecology, biology, health sciences, and other applied physical sciences ... abstain from expressing serious concern about ... the splendid isolation in which academic economics now finds itself.'[260] Professor Leontiev's complaint is the 'nearly irresistible predilection for deductive reasoning'.[261]

In the face of such criticism, it is hard to sustain any claim that free market economics has any scientific status. When they create new aircraft, physicists, engineers and designers don't need to argue about the basic principles because these have been verified again and again in laboratory experiments. There are no Nobel prize winners warning of fatal flaws in the assumptions being used. There may well be practical disagreements about how a new design will perform, but these will be settled by building models, testing them in wind tunnels and flying actual prototypes. All the time, aerodynamic theory will thus be undergoing rigorous testing against reality.

At this stage, it is only fair to point out that, even *within* the prevailing orthodoxy, there are leading economists who understand the limitations of their abstract theories as a guide to the real world. For example, the Theory of Second Best undermines any uncritical faith in free markets. According to Lipsey and Lancaster,[262] removing just a few 'distortions' would not necessarily make any given market work better. Such intervention could even worsen its performance. In our context, for example, the absence of textbook purity ensures that no-one can have *any* idea whether the various forms of Open Skies regime would work better, even than the most rigid traditional bilaterals. On this reasoning, 'New' Labour's preferred model could produce something vastly inferior.

Free market theory also has serious problems with transport networks. People may place a high value on having a comprehensive public transport system – even if they rarely use it! But there is no way that a community can register this preference in a market. We pay for tickets when we actually want to travel. Long ago, to give him credit, Alfred Kahn[263] recognised that markets cannot present users with a *strategic* choice: 'should we build a transport network, and of what type and quality?' Such complex systems can only develop out of *collective* decisions.[264]

It may come as a surprise that even some Chicago economists admit that competition doesn't work in certain situations. Suppose the demand for a good is periodic or uncertain, its production units large in relation to individual demand, and unsold stocks are 'perishable'. These are leading characteristics of scheduled air networks. Professor Lester G Telser explains that, in such cases, there will inevitably be some uneconomic pricing, and profitability will be elusive. He concludes that: 'Eventually ... the situation gets so bad that very drastic reforms are necessary.' What sort of reforms? 'Players in the game should 'co-operate' to achieve economic efficiency.' That is, producers must set 'the total capacity that society needs and agree on prices that will achieve efficiency.'[265]

This highly respectable American economist is declaring that, in these circumstances, the only way to efficiency is through some kind of 'collusion'. And that, he explains, can be public ownership, regulation or co-operation among producers. Telser firmly believes in competition where it is feasible but, in this case, his mathematical analysis has driven him to a non-competitive solution. American anti-trust lawyers have been quick to spot that 'this work strikes at the root of orthodox economic doctrine.'[266]

Professor Frank Hahn (not to be confused with Alfred Kahn) offers a balanced overview: 'The limitations on the applicability of pure market theory are numerous and some of them are quite serious ... Our knowledge of the actual movements of the [Invisible] hand is rudimentary and vastly incomplete ... The Smithian vision ... can be dangerously misleading when this limited role is not recognised.' With 'public goods', Hahn believes 'the market economy will perform disastrously.' As for environmental problems, he is clear that 'one cannot ascribe failures of the invisible hand in the face of externalities exclusively to defective property rights.' Professor Hahn's general conclusion is that 'on purely logical considerations, as well as on the basis of quite simple observations, the invisible hand is likely to be unsure in its operation and occasionally downright arthritic ...'[267]

Economies which significantly depart from perfect competition – that is, 'most real world economies' – should therefore be 'candidates for the deployment of a visible hand'. Hahn suggests that a 'step by step, case by case approach ... seems to be the only reasonable one in economic policy.'[268] There is nothing here to underpin 'New' Labour's assertions about the superiority of 'the market'. But perhaps the 'New Economy' is changing everything so radically that we need to think things out afresh.

Has The 'New' Economy Rendered Our Existing View Of Aviation Obsolete?

The 'New Economy', a somewhat vague concept, is said to be based on information technology.[269] It is believed to usher in higher productivity, lower inflation and faster growth – providing that radical new policies are deployed to realise the potential. These policies can eliminate 'boom and bust cycles', make markets work 'more dynamically, and encourage investment in technology, innovation, skills and infrastructure'.[270]

Achieving long term macro-economic stability, such as 'New' Labour promises, would greatly benefit air transport. In all recorded history, however, it is hard to find any sustained period when economic dynamism has been combined with stable growth and steady prices.[271] As the doyen of business cycle research, Professor Victor Zarnowitz, points out: 'Those who see business cycle recessions as a thing of the past cannot boast of superior knowledge ... [they are] mostly commentators on current events. Yet they are predicting a radical shift from historical trend cycle patterns.'[272] In other words, there is no serious basis for this optimistic view.

Depressions are now supposed to be a thing of the past, because of the great thrust in productivity brought about by information technology. Charles Leadbeater, a formative influence[273] on 'New' Labour, claims that the whole nature of the economy is changing. He believes that 'Most of us ... [are] in the thin air business.'[274] Policies should therefore be geared to the new 'weightless' economy where most of us are buying and selling intangible products. This calls for a new wave of 'radical innovation in many of our most basic political, social, and economic institutions.' This includes privatisation of hospitals, schools and other public services.[275] Leadbeater accordingly thinks that Tony Blair is 'not modernising enough'.[276]

It is true that, in the 1990s, the rate of growth of annual productivity doubled in the USA. During that time, computers were invading almost every sphere. Their use in 'Just-In-Time' industrial systems probably damped down the violent swings in goods and materials stocks that play a part in business cycles. But according to the most detailed analysis, by Professor R J Gordon, the contribution of information technology to the productivity spurt was 'a mere pittance'.[277] Gordon gives most credit to the 1990s cyclical upturn, and to technological changes in factories producing durable goods, such as aircraft. There was indeed a great deal of IT investment, but much of it was once-and-for-all in nature. And there is no sign at all of the US economy becoming *dominated* by 'weightless', high-tech firms which 'network' together in flexible, ever-changing, alliances.[278]

Will the great projected growth of air traffic spawn a proliferation of such 'weightless' activities, which will call for Mr. Leadbeater's radical policy innovations? We may expect many new firms, specialising in areas like software development, aircraft interior design and on-board entertainment. Fresh 'niches' will be developed, such as personalised business transport, new kinds of package holiday and varieties of scenic or thrill flying. No doubt also, many new firms will try to break into mainstream aviation in rivalry with the MegaCarriers. There is no need to dwell on the fate awaiting most of them.

No doubt many 'weightless' businesses will emerge, some of a kind we can't yet imagine. But the Internet, far from being a great leveller as many believe, has armed MegaBusiness (not merely airlines) with a great new doomsday weapon. Entire sectors, like the retail travel trade, may soon struggle barely to survive, as airlines sell their tickets directly to the public. That they have always been 'weightless' won't help them much. Although its technology may be more exciting, the dynamics of the New Economy may thus not be very different from the capitalism we already know. Indeed, the Secretary of State for Trade and Industry recently admitted that the ideas on which 'New' Labour's policy for the knowledge economy rested are 'mistaken'. According to Patricia Hewitt, 'The idea of Living on Thin Air was so much hot air'.[279]

This is somewhat unfair on Mr. Leadbeater who identifies some interesting trends, even if he leaves room for debate about their overall significance. For example, some airlines have explored the concept of a 'virtual' operation where the only 'core' employees are senior managers plus those, like cabin crew and check-in staff, who deal directly with the public. 'Non-core' labour could be employed from wherever costs were lowest. Many 'weightless' office functions could well be performed thousands of miles away from base. Aircraft could be 'wet leased', i.e. rented, complete with flight crews, from Flag of Convenience countries. Some airlines will push as far as they dare in this direction. They will be encouraged by 'New' Labour's enthusiasm for global market forces. Related to this is the concept of 'labour market flexibility'.

Is 'Labour Market Flexibility' A Good Thing For Air Transport?

Promoting such 'flexibility' is a central plank in Tony Blair's campaign to 'reform' the European Union.[280] But as Professor Robert M Solow has observed, 'labour market rigidity' is never defined precisely "but only by the enumeration of tell-tale symptoms".[281] These include a feeling' that unemployment benefits are 'too high', that trade unions are too strong and that labour market regulations ought to be scrapped. Consistently with this, 'New' Labour has opposed the European Union's attempts to limit, e.g. the maximum working hours of road haulage drivers. As we write, the European Commission is 'threatening' Britain with legal action because the UK has not activated a Directive on length of the working week.[282] For Mr. Blair, these are decisions best left to 'markets'.

Air transport has much experience of what this means in practice. As pointed out earlier, many US 'new entrants' benefited from a general surplus of high quality labour. Many ground staff at PeoplExpress, for example, were unemployed medical personnel.[283] A large proportion of their earnings varied with company profits. In the absence of unions, hiring and firing was also highly 'flexible'. PeoplExpress was thus able to achieve labour costs perhaps a third of those of the established Major carriers. This, of course, is why 'labour market flexibility' is so attractive to employers.

How the established American carriers responded varied with the state of their internal labour relations. There was a general drive towards 'multi-tasking', more flexible practices, part time working, reduced social benefits and, most controversial of all, 'two tier' pay systems. Under the latter, newly recruited staff members would, throughout their careers, earn less for identical work than colleagues recruited an earlier date. It isn't hard to imagine the tensions this provoked. Continental Airlines went to extremes of 'flexibilisation' after its first emergence from bankruptcy. Later, the airline became insolvent a second time. Many airline people believe that this was due to a steep decline in service quality. The airline paid the price of low staff morale.

During the nineties, however, this flexibility increasingly turned sour as the US labour market tightened. The low wage operators started losing employees. Because of staff hostility, major airlines quietly began removing the 'two-tier' pay systems. We have already discussed what happened at carriers like North West, TWA and United, where labour exchanged work 'concessions' for shares and seats on the board. More recently, there has been a tendency for unions to 'claw back' many of those concessions. In recent years, staff earnings at most US airlines have been rising strongly.

The lesson of experience is clear: no airline can hope for success without a highly skilled, broadly educated and well motivated labour force, ready to adapt quickly to changing circumstances. That means a heavy investment in people. It makes no sense not to use those human resources to their full potential, or let them drift elsewhere. Long term job security, civilised treatment, and honest involvement of the work force in decision making is essential for success. This has little or nothing in common with Tony Blair's kind of 'labour market flexibility'.

But perhaps we are looking at this through specialised spectacles. 'New' Labour's view is that such flexibility benefits everyone by leading to a 'high rate of employment'. This notion is based on an ancient dogma to the effect that 'There will always be a tendency at work for wage rates to be so related to demand that everybody is employed';[284] and that workers should 'learn to submit to declines of money income without squealing'.[285] Once again, we should note that leading modern theorists, like Professors Hahn and Solow, have shown that 'full nominal wage flexibility would bring with it enough other problems to make it a non-solution to the problem of unemployment'.[286]

The shakiness of the orthodox position was exposed by the Organisation for Economic Co-operation and Developments's own economists. They showed that there was 'little or no association' between the 'strictness' of employment legislation and overall unemployment. Their political chiefs rushed out a press release in an attempt to confuse the issue.[287] Professor Solow analysed jobless statistics in relation to actual vacancies. He reached conclusions 'squarely against the cliché that persistent European unemployment is entirely or mainly a matter of "labour market rigidities".'[288] On Solow's measure, French and German performance is much superior to that of the USA, and particularly the UK.[289] Even where Blair's nostrum is supposed to work best – in creating jobs for the young, unskilled, and less educated – 'flexible' countries like America and Britain do 'no better, and frequently far worse' than allegedly 'rigid' countries.[290]

Tony Blair's position looks even less tenable in wider perspective. Ever since the mid-seventies, it has become progressively more difficult for European workers, including those in aviation, to take collective action to further their interests. In many countries, real wages have tended to stagnate.[291] Job insecurity has grown, while social benefits have been whittled down. With the erosion of social protection, increasing labour market flexibility has gone hand in hand with a lengthening dole queue. Lack of flexibility thus surely cannot be the main explanation for European unemployment. The best analytical work suggests that the most likely reason is tight fiscal and monetary policy. The Maastricht Treaty directly affects each EU country's output and employment, as they strive to meet its fiscal targets. With closer integration, and capital market globalisation, this downward pressure tends to be accentuated. Macro economic forces thus appear to be the prime cause of the European dole queue, although one careful analysis debits increasing world competition with around a fifth of the rise in unemployment.[292]

We can only agree with Gordon Brown that Britain 'has been the laboratory for [labour market] deregulation in Europe', but it 'will not work and ought not to be continued.' These wise remarks were published in a book entitled 'Beware The US Model'.[293] Nowadays, Mr. Brown is more in favour of 'lifting regulatory burdens'. In particular, he appears to have a mystical faith in the potential role of small firms, once they are freed of 'red tape'. This issue is of such importance to air transport that we must look at his case, even at the risk of repeating ourselves.

Does Preferential Treatment For Small Firms Boost Economic Efficiency?

Small firms, the argument goes, have created many millions of new jobs across the entire US economy. It follows that they could do the same in Europe. Unfortunately, this is based on another case of Statistical Myopia. While it is true that small firms have created large numbers of jobs, it is also true that they have 'destroyed' nearly as many.[294] In the bargain, small companies tend to pay their workers less, and seldom offer pensions, health insurance or employment security. That is even the case in Silicon Valley where nearly half the workers are classified as semi- or unskilled. Their pay is low, and fringe benefits usually non-existent.[295]

It may be a laudable aim to help small companies, but government should be clear about what it is trying to do. The Americans have undoubtedly been successful with small high-tech 'start ups'. However, the key measures were not designed to drive down workers' earnings. They related to finance, infrastructure plus research and development. According to Dr John Schmitt of the Economic Policy Institute, 'It is public investment and research subsidies that have given US high tech firms a head start over their competitors'.[296] 'Reducing red tape', he points out, merely cuts down on protection for users. Letting small firms ignore labour standards brings about further erosion of pay and working conditions, while putting employers who treat workers fairly at a disadvantage. Schmitt concludes that the 'deregulation of product and labour markets is almost completely irrelevant for high-tech ventures and potentially dangerous for everybody else.'[297]

This is certainly true for aviation, particularly any relaxation of finance, fitness and safety standards. Under classical UK regulation, it was accepted that small newcomers could inject some fresh ideas into the industry. British policy therefore used to encourage new airlines to develop within protected niches, e.g. as regional or charter operators. The survivors might later seek to operate on prime scheduled routes. If they were unfairly attacked, they could be protected. But without regulation, it is hard for them to survive. This presents free market economists with a dilemma. Competition authorities in Europe have compelled certain airlines to co-operate with their supposed competitors, e.g. by accepting their tickets. The most remarkable case is where a German court refused to let Lufthansa match the tariffs of a newcomer, Germania.[298] Never before has such airline fare matching been prevented.

However strong the theoretical belief in market forces, when the prospective casualties are smaller private companies, enthusiasm for the elimination contest tends to fall away. What is emerging in Europe, without those concerned apparently grasping its significance, is something tending towards the US gridiron football leagues. These have elaborate methods to ensure that weaker teams are given a helping hand. That could well be a sensible policy for airlines too, but it has little to do with the free market axioms that drive policy making in London and Brussels. Thus once again, in the name of 'competition', we see the introduction of detailed controls.

Classical regulators could deal with such problems in a more sensible way. Take the emergence of the new 'low fare' scheduled airlines. Given the evolution of air travel, with long term growth mainly in 'leisure' categories, these operations have been slow to develop. More than fifteen years ago, the aviation trade unions tried to persuade certain British airlines to set up an ultra-low cost subsidiary – the People's Skybus.[299] Partly because of the source of the concept, it was firmly rejected. But the main reason was undoubtedly mental inertia, reinforced by a short term focus on profitability. It was left to 'new entrants' to develop the idea. Some years later, they did so. Now the European low fare operators are expanding, while more traditional scheduled airlines are feeling the draught. The possibility looms of a bloody confrontation between MegaCarriers and the upstarts.

This will happen if the latter emerge from their niche routes between 'secondary' airports to confront their bigger rivals head on, as did PeoplExpress. The resulting conflict will call for sophisticated regulation. Public policy should favour the wider availability of low scheduled fares for the mass of people. This is bound to mean an enhanced share of intra-European traffic for the low fare operators. Those airlines should be protected from unfair attack by the MegaCarriers. That could easily be done, using tried and tested techniques. without placing artificial handicaps on the big airlines. To help keep a balance, there should also be strong action against misleading advertising and selling practices. Regulators could easily publish some objective information.[300] Most people would regard all this as common sense. Blair's philosophy rules it out.

'New' Labour's ideas on small firms thus have their limitations. In particular, they have no room for publicly owned small firms like Inmos which produced the brilliantly successful Transputer.[301] This is symptomatic of a general lack of knowledge of the most important modernising trends in world industry. Three of them are highly relevant to aviation.

What Are The Real Dynamics Of Industrial Modernisation?

The world's most successful firms achieved their present status by ignoring the maxims of text book competition. Standard US business histories, like those by Professor Alfred Chandler, illustrate this with such revealing titles as 'The Visible Hand'.[302] As Professor William Lazonick stresses, the 'essential weapon' of big business has been, and still is, *organisational* capability. Crucial to its success is a privileged, i.e. non-market, access to resources.[303] As we saw, this is true of the airlines, who seek full control over their route structures and distribution systems. Whatever the external pressures on them, it is hard to find successful major firms which generally rely on market mechanisms to co-ordinate their own operations.[304]

In recent times, Japanese firms have evolved the most advanced practices, and their experience underlines the value of co-operation between groups of firms, as opposed to cut throat market relationships.[305] Planning by the Ministry of International Trade and Industry (MITI) has also played a creative role in the remarkable success of Japanese industry. The tendency for industrial leadership to shift from the United States to Japan was a transition from a highly organised managerial capitalism to an even more highly organised collective capitalism. This was complemented by a degree of state planning and co-ordination.[306] The present difficulties of Japan are, in large part, due to the fact that these policies have been too successful.[307]

The most dynamic US industries are now following the same approach. For example, Boeing is revolutionising aircraft production with techniques adapted from Japanese car manufacturing.[308] A central feature is a continuously moving assembly line, not before seen in modern aircraft production. In a 'just-in-time' approach, Boeing is striving for ever-closer integration with its suppliers and customers. This sophisticated new policy, Boeing stresses, would not be possible without the full involvement, and co-operation, of the company's work force. The great technological drive doesn't come from 'weightless' subcontractors. It originates in the company's 'Phantom Works' in which 4,000 scientists and engineers pursue 'breakthrough improvements'. This is where public support is fed into the industry.

But 'New' Labour believes that 'only business can create wealth'.[309] This makes it hard to explain how the word processor producing these lines ever came to exist. According to a US history of personal computing, the 'foundations were laid by the government' and 'in reality, the story didn't start with these young entrepreneurs' [such as Bill Gates of Microsoft][310] It all started when the US Navy financed the Whirlwind computer to build a flight simulator, thus opening research into interactive techniques. The SAGE early warning system, mentioned earlier, became the 'pipeline that transported Whirlwind's technology into the commercial world.' From there, the Pentagon sponsored the invention of the mouse, on screen windows, laser printers, area networks and ultimately the Internet.[311]

The reality is that the US federal state supports sections of American industry, not just aviation, on a breathtaking scale.[312] This is justified by the argument that adequate defence is only possible if US industry is at the leading edge of world technology. 'Strategic' sectors are targeted and 'Buy American' policies enforced. Civil and military institutions go well beyond the provision of research funds. For example, the military supported the development of integrated circuits until costs had been driven down to a point where civil applications became fully economic. However it is dressed up, this is purposive planning. No surprise that, according to the US National Academy of Sciences, the 'federal government has played a critical role in supporting research that underlies computer-based products and services'.[313]

The US government thus drives long range projects that private industry cannot, or will not, sustain. It is always ready to create new organisations or challenge the views of private business. For example, when IBM dropped its work on relational databases, the National Science Foundation stepped in.[314] Whatever we think of the Americans' political motives, the undeniable fact is that all this is happening, and it works. Current programmes will drive Information Technology to entirely new levels, with astonishingly wide effects. In the long term, for example, the main beneficiary of Virtual 3D reality – three dimension graphic images for military simulators – will probably be Hollywood. If Mr. Leadbeater's 'weightless world' comes about, it will have been made possible by military bureaucrats. Whitehall knows government 'can't pick winners'. The US military does it all the time.

And finally, what should be the most obvious truth of all for a Labour government. It simply isn't true that a cowed labour force is essential for modern industrial success. The experience of many US 'high performance' companies[315] demonstrates that most success is achieved when managers share their power, and when workers are given some serious discretion. This was shown in a study of steel, textile, medical electronics and imaging plants. If allowed some initiative, self-directed workers can make a huge contribution to the success of operations. This leads to a happier work force, and can unleash much creativity. But it is hard for such relations to emerge in a situation of all-out competition. The more cut throat the product market, the more aggressive managers tend to be. They have to satisfy their shareholders. The more 'flexible' the labour market, the less able workers are to defend their interests. And then, as we see today at some famous airlines, the worse the outcome for all concerned.

After sifting all this evidence, we arrive at an unavoidable conclusion. To the extent that they have any substance at all, 'New' Labour's modernising ideas are based on ancient dogmas. Far from being self-evidently true, Tony Blair's philosophy is of little or no use as a guide to the complex dynamics of modern industry. Policy makers could probably do as well with the help of Old Moore's Almanack.

- *Tony Blair's 'modernising' political strategy may be effective in winning elections but it brings a short termist, and often subjective, approach to policy making, rather than thorough analysis as a basis for tackling problems at root.*
- *The vacuum created by 'New' Labour's failure to develop realistic economic policies has been filled by the simplistic dogmas of 'free market' orthodoxy, and this is leading to irrational policy decisions.*
- *The concept of the 'New' Economy has little substance and, to the extent that the aviation industry becomes increasingly 'weightless', this will reinforce the powerful tendency towards industrial concentration.*
- *Labour market flexibility does not bring the benefits Tony Blair claims for it, in terms of job creation, technological innovation or the creation of civilised workplace relations.*
- *'New' Labour's emphasis on small firms is out of proportion to their significance, and 'cutting red tape' is dangerous in air transport, where the potential strengths of small operators can best be realised under strong regulation.*
- *Tony Blair's notions are a hotch potch of political calculation, journalistic 'spin' and ancient economic dogmas which could never stand up in fair and open debate, and their application to air transport is harming the industry.*

Chapter Seven
Reorientation: A Realistic Strategy for the Modern World?

Tony Blair has set some intriguing puzzles for future historians. 'New' Labour came to power long after it had become obvious that Market Theology was a disastrous failure as a basis for economic policy. The official economists may cling to their faith, supported by various 'Think Tanks', financial journalists and consultancy firms. But worldly politicians must surely understand what rubbish it is, and how poor the results have been from applying it. Otherwise, there would be no need at all to 'massage' official statistics, conceal data on phoney grounds of 'commercial confidentiality' or make personal attacks on critics, while ignoring their criticisms.

As in Hans Andersen's story, 'New' Labour's courtiers jostle each other to admire what they have been told are the fashionable robes tailored for the Emperor in Chicago, Washington and Wapping. Anyone who can't see the brilliant cloth, with its gossamer Third Way trimmings, is unfit for office, out of date or just plain stupid. As always with the latest fashions, the styling must be exactly right. So no-one expects to see such labels as Enron, Railtrack, NATS or deregulated Californian electricity.[316] As for growing social inequality, the economic ruin inflicted on so many countries by the International Monetary Fund, and the threat of environmental catastrophe ... these contemporary designs are not allowed anywhere near the imperial wardrobe. It will be recalled that a little boy blurted out that the Emperor wore no clothes. But the analogy lacks perfection, because a sensitive part of the 'New' Labour Emperor's anatomy is in fact covered up. As with all codpieces, this has the dual effect of both concealing, and drawing attention to, whatever is hidden beneath. What could it possibly be?

What Is Hidden Beneath The Emperor's Codpiece?
A few questions may help us solve the puzzle. For example, why does 'New' Labour, however damning the evidence that UK railway privatisation is a complete failure, veto any measure for reabsorbing the system into the public sector?[317] Or even criticise the principle of

rail privatisation? All the government needs do is take back, at no cost, the Train Operating Franchises as they expire. Why does Blair prefer immense subsidies to private interests instead of the cheaper and more efficient course of public ownership or control? Why did he, against all disinterested advice, force through his policy on NATS? Privatisation was bound to fail. The collapse took only a month or two to happen. Given this abysmal record, why does the government still assure foreign countries that privatisation is an outstanding success?[318]

We can't blame focus groups or opinion surveys because the great majority of people dislike these policies. Only one answer makes any sense. It must be an overriding priority for 'New' Labour to further the interests of British financial services, and those of business generally. There are big profits for the City in privatising public enterprises, and there are many inviting targets in foreign countries. Certain types of British firm will be able to export their know-how in cutting wages, reducing service quality and squeezing out profits. That is the basis of Tony Blair's campaign for European Union 'reform'. It is also an effective way of currying favour with the international capital markets, which have made so much out of past UK privatisations.

Such interests perceive Britain as a safe haven in an uncertain world. For private business abhors any regulation that constrains its decisions. It looks for attractive and reasonably guaranteed profits. 'New' Labour's PFI/PPP drive is faithfully striving to deliver these. No wonder that Blair is at pains to avoid any policies, or even rhetoric, which international markets could interpret as a 'shift to the Left'. For that might 'downgrade the UK economy as an investment proposition'.[319] 'New' Labour's aim is to keep foreign investment flowing into Britain. That inflow, it is hoped, will help the government to keep UK interest rates down.

Since 'New' Labour's thoughts first moved in this direction, it has become even more business-friendly. There is no need for us to give chapter and verse because readers will be well aware of what is happening from the newspapers. In business terms, Blair has 'repositioned' the Labour Party in the political 'market place'. He is trying to cement the support of a new social base, while doing just enough to keep Labour's traditional supporters 'on board'. But the costs of doing this are stupifyingly high. Even so, it is doubtful whether

'New' Labour can buy the long term support of private business. This is a fickle constituency, always looking for the highest bidder. Only an unremitting stream of favours will retain its support. It is true that past Labour governments also looked for co-operation with the private sector. But that is very different from uncritically assuming that 'What's Good For International Business Is Always Best For Britain'.

Modernisation should instead be about strategies that are Relevant, Workable and Superior. Relevant in that they tackle real structural problems. Workable in that they are based on global best practice. Superior in that they improve the lives of the majority of people.

A Modernising Strategy For The Third Millennium?

Our analysis has suggested modern policies for each sector of air transport. When we put them together, they clearly point in one strategic direction. A comprehensive strategy for mainstream Labour would require a view much wider than that of one industry, however important. However, we suggest that any genuine Modernisation would include the following components.

1. Effective strategies can only flow out of realistic analysis of the powerful forces now reshaping societies throughout the world. Global economic dynamics are having an enormous impact, but they are not the entire story. Many substantial changes taking place are the outcome of *political* choices. The small print of treaties, laws and regulations is everywhere being rewritten to facilitate private business, and to stop governments from 'interfering' with its transactions. 'New' Labour claims there is no alternative but to *submit* to 'globalisation'. But nation states and, even more so, blocs like the European Union, still have significant room for manoeuvre. *A modern approach would reject economic and political fatalism. It would carefully assess the scope for taking conscious democratic control over these forces.*

2. Today's mass media are dominated by fleeting images, 'sound bites' and trivial ephemera. This imparts a powerful bias towards over simplification. Political discourse is conducted in slogans like 'sleepy bureaucracy' versus 'free market dynamism'. A serious treatment of issues would explain complex background, put things in context and draw reasoned conclusions. This can't readily be

done in sound bite brevity, so the scales are heavily loaded against informed debate. In this light, 'New' Labour's heavy use of media 'spin' is, to some extent, forgivable. What is wholly unacceptable is Blair's refusal, or inability, to engage in any other kind of discourse, even with his own supporters. *A modern approach would encourage informed, honest and open debate. This is essential to the health of a political party. Moreover, it can help save governments from policy debacles like those with the London Underground and National Air Traffic Services.*

3. 'New' Labour's failure to engage in systematic thinking has created a policy vacuum which has been filled, at operational level, by Market Theology. Regardless of circumstances, Blair's policy conclusions almost always boil down to the same handful of simplistic nostrums. Official documents are now so predictable that we know what they will say before we even open the pages. The necessary qualifications for official authorship do not appear to include the ability to distinguish a Boeing 747 from a wheelbarrow. This theological approach is now spreading via Brussels to other countries of continental Europe. As a consequence, almost any suggestion of constructive action is liable to be dismissed as producing a 'market distortion'. In the past, mainstream Labour would have ridiculed such nonsense. *A modern approach would reject Market Theology. It would instead stimulate creative socialist thinking. The aim would be to develop a realistic philosophy for the Third Millennium.*

4. When Mrs. Thatcher's power was at its height, competition in air transport was *not* seen as 'an end in itself'. It was instead a 'valuable mechanism' for securing certain objectives[320] and only then 'in the right circumstances.' In the bargain, 'short term gains in user satisfaction ... [had to] be weighed against the longer term need for the sound development of an efficient and competitive industry, on which the continuing satisfaction of user demand must depend.' Airlines couldn't rest on their laurels, because there should always be 'at least one airline fit and able to replace [an] incumbent operator wherever the need for substitution may arise.'[321] Under Tony Blair things are much more simplistic. The Civil Aviation Authority single mindedly promotes 'liberalisation through the removal of Government imposed restrictions on entry

to the airline market'.[322] Just one mechanism now, for all conceivable situations. It is time to return to more realistic policies and take account of wider factors, including the environment. *A modern approach would begin by working out objectives. Only then would it decide what mechanisms could best achieve them.*

5. Historically, Europe developed star-shaped air route structures, based on hubs in the various nation states. That significantly limited operational efficiency.[323] By scrapping nationalistic restrictions, EU deregulation was supposed to 'open things up'. Instead the Single Market is leading to even tighter hub-with-spokes structures. For the MegaCarriers are well aware that, the closer an industry resembles the free market ideal, the more it suffers from instability and over production. 'Competition' having produced such modest results, the authorities indulge in *ad hoc* interventionism, some of which makes little sense. There should be aviation specific *professional* regulators who can, where necessary, deploy countervailing power against MegaCarriers in the interests of the travelling public. They could also protect those operators that achieve ultra-low costs by legitimate means. Such policies are now ruled out on theological grounds. *A modern approach would take account of realities. It would downgrade Competition Policy in favour of aviation-specific regulation. And it would create a specialised Civil Aviation Authority for the whole of Europe.*

6. The costs of 'natural monopolies' and regulated industries tend to fall over the long term.[324] Whereas fragmented markets are unable to plan coherent networks, monopolies like the American Telephone and Telegraph Company were able to do so, with great success.[325] It thus is far from true that only 'free competition' leads to greater efficiency and better service to the public. In many industries, it inflates such costs as marketing, sales and product differentiation, while it simultaneously ratchets down pay rates, staffing levels and service quality. This pressures firms, which can 'establish' themselves in any EU country, into treating their employees in less humane ways. Trade unions, on the other hand, are hampered from organising on an EU scale, and are thus at a disadvantage. EU policies also work against any form of industrial diversity or experiment. They rule out job creation enterprises, fail

to help non-commercial entities like Co-ops, and undermine vital public 'monopolies' like post offices, railways and urban transport networks. The European Union regime is thus weighted towards private business and against the public interest. *A modern approach would reject unrestrained competition in favour of a managed regime. It would stress the importance of minimum social standards. It would develop a diverse range of institutions, particularly those which transcend the narrow horizons of private business.*

7. Privatisation is supposed to lower costs, spawn many little businesses and maximise competition. It rarely does any of these things.[326] Where privatisation can't be achieved, the European Commission insists on the 'commercial investor' principle. But public bodies often serve a wide social purpose. For example, the managerial decisions of British Airways, British Airports and National Air Traffic Services have serious implications for the entire UK economy. Their business is not private business. It is public business. As such operations become internationalised, the need for social accountability becomes even more acute. Strong regulation will go so far. A better answer will often be international public ownership. This could readily be brought about at European Union level. It would, for example, be a natural way of achieving the Single European Sky, using the present Eurocontrol as a nucleus. Public enterprise already reaches across national frontiers. When Tony Blair switches on a light in Downing Street, the power comes from a French public enterprise. As for more than one country working together, the three Scandinavian governments built up a successful airline. In truth, the possibilities are limitless. That would be *real* European integration. *A modern approach would firmly reject the theological belief that private firms offer the sole route to EU integration. It would sponsor a major role for co-operative and public enterprises, both national and international. And the European Union would itself, where appropriate, create supranational enterprises.*

8. The transport infrastructure of the American economy was built up with lavish support from the US Federal state. The USA still gives colossal support to its advanced industries. No nonsense here about 'leaving it to market forces'. European integration could benefit dramatically by adopting US style industrial policies,

particularly with infrastructure. For example, it is fifteen years since the Sunrise Europe[327] proposal for a pan-European broad band network was floated. There is still no sign whatever that 'free enterprise' will produce it. And yet, such a project would be a tremendous step towards the Information SuperHighway, stimulate computing in all its forms, and have a revolutionary impact on transport systems. Instead of the idiotic drive for postal 'competition', there could be a high-tech, ultra-reliable, universal public service. 'Star Wars' technology could be focused on Europe's railways, raising their capacity, automating freight movement and extending ultra high speed passenger services. The barriers are not technical. They are political and theological. *A modern approach would emulate the Americans. It would mobilise the European Union to push through dynamic industrial policies. The aim would be to lift Europe to wholly new levels of technology and productivity.*

9. Making full use of its power, the USA can usually ensure that smaller countries accommodate their policies to American needs. 'Free' market regimes, such as Open Skies, are one of the most effective weapons for achieving US aims. The interests of European countries are, of course, often quite different. Individually, most of them find it hard to counter American power. United in a bloc, Europe could stand up to the USA. Aerospace offers graphic proof of what is possible, in the shape of the successful Airbus series. Europe could also exert much more influence over the generality of international market forces. If it did so, Europe could play a much more constructive role on the world political scene. *A modern approach would harness the European Union's vast bargaining potential. Negotiating as a bloc would enable Europe to balance American economic and political power.*

10. 'New' Labour appears to believe that deregulation, marketisation and privatisation are the only rational responses to globalisation. In aviation, as in other sectors, we have shown that this is simply not true. Tony Blair favours the dismantling of national economic controls. But he is not suggesting anything in their place. In no sense, however, is it in the interests of the majority of people for nation states to discard their regulatory powers until there are effective mechanisms for the social governance of international

business. In aviation, as in other sectors, the prime objective should be a managed regime, under full democratic control. The European Union can make a start by creating its own such mechanisms. It can also use its considerable power to work towards the creation of wider world institutions. *A modern approach would note the potential of a truly global economy. But it would also understand that the potential can only be realised if economic forces are adequately managed. It would see no merit in dismantling national controls until satisfactory mechanisms had been created at international level.*

* * * * *

As we write, Tony Blair is insisting on the 'liberalisation' of British media ownership rules.[328] This will allow foreign interests to add television channels to their UK newspaper empires. The 'deal' Blair is said to be offering would require, as a *quid pro quo*, support for a Yes vote in a Euro referendum. Such a campaign would no doubt enable 'New' Labour to replenish its coffers with yet more funds from private business.[329] This further Americanisation of our television raises profound cultural, political and social issues. They are outside our present scope, so we simply note that, as with 'Open Skies', the Americans would never give similar privileges to foreigners within the USA. This is codpiece politics at its most blatant.

Which reminds us that codpieces have often served an important political purpose. Edward III had a suit of armour with a truly monstrous projection. It was supposed to frighten away his battle opponents, particularly peasant soldiers. At the climax of the fashion, Henry VIII wore a jewel studded specimen, so immense that it was said to enter a room before he did. For well known reasons, Henry wanted to impress foreign ambassadors with his apparent virility. But his codpiece also covered evidence of the serious disease that created grave problems for the Tudor succession.[330] That disease was a key factor in the chain of events leading to Henry's massive privatisation drive, out of which many 'new' Fat Cats made their fortunes.

It would be unhistorical to draw modern parallels, but Tony Blair's 'project' reminds us of some classical themes. Karl Marx is supposed to be out of date but 'New' Labour is surely working towards turning the British government into the 'executive committee of the bourgeoisie'.[331] No political imperative forces Blair down this path, for Labour would easily have won power in 1997, under almost any leader or manifesto.[332] Yes, we recognise the great strength of world economic forces. But there is a world of difference between realism and fatalism. Deregulation, marketisation and privatisation are far from inevitable consequences of globalisation. They are not dictated by impersonal forces from outside. On the contrary, they flow from conscious political decisions. And they are imposed 'from above'.

Nine out of ten Londoners are reported to oppose privatisation of the Underground infrastructure. That is the extent to which people are aware of the Emperor's sartorial condition. Blair urgently needs to employ some modern tailors. He won't meet them in City board rooms or at Washington cocktail parties. He should take advantage of mainstream Labour's experience, knowledge and wisdom. That would help him avoid such grave errors as creating Railtracks in the sky. In aviation, as elsewhere, 'New' Labour should instead be promoting the broad interests of the industry, the people who work in it, the travelling public, the wider population and the natural environment. The British government, together with partners in Europe, should be working to bring the vast, and often destructive, forces of the world 'market' under conscious social control.

It is time to recognise the obvious: 'New' Labour has failed. A major reorientation of strategy is urgently required. To achieve that, mainstream Labour must reassert itself, and do so on a European basis. There must be an end to codpiece politics. It's high time for some genuine modernisation. Nothing less will do.

Notes and References

1   Department of the Environment, Transport and the Regions (DETR), 'The Future of Aviation: the Government's Consultation Document on Air Transport Policy', 12 December 2000. (Henceforth, CDATP). Since this was published, DETR has twice been reorganised and renamed.

2   Such terminology appears in official pronouncements, e.g. by Sir Malcolm Field, Chairman, Civil Aviation Authority in his 'A Single Global Aviation Market' of 1999. We are indebted to CAA for this.

3   CDATP, Chapter Two, para 27.

4   Advice of the Director General of Fair Trading to the Secretary of State for Trade and Industry (then Peter Mandelson) on the 'Proposed Alliance Between British Airways and American Airlines', published as enclosure to DTI press notice of 8 August 1998.

5   DETR consultation paper, 'A Public Private Partnership For National Air Traffic Services Ltd' (NATS), October 1998.

6   H M Treasury White Paper, 'Realising Europe's Potential: Economic Reform in Europe', HMSO, Cmnd 5318, February 2002.

7   Professor Kahn was Chairman of the Civil Aeronautics Board during the process of deregulation, and its most vociferous advocate. Kahn was later US 'Inflation Czar', and presided over a spectacular inflation. See his 'The Macroeconomic Consequences of Sensible Microeconomic Policies', The First Distinguished Lecture on Economics in Government, Dallas, December 1984.

8   H. G. Wells, 'Anticipations', Chapman and Hall, London, 1902, Chapter I, page 32.

9   For example, 'The advent of civil air transport in Britain and Europe was a direct outcome of the First World War', in R. Higham, 'Britain's Imperial Air Routes, 1918 to 1939', Foulis, London, 1960.

10 Air Transport Association, 'The Airline Handbook – Online Version', Chapter 1, 'Dawn of the Jet Age: Government and Technology in the USA', at www.air-transport.org

11 Jean Guinet and Dirk Pilat, 'Promoting innovation – does it matter?', OECD Observer 217/8, Summer edition 1999.

12 Arthur D. Little Ltd., 'Study into the Potential Impact of Changes in Technology on the Development of Air Transport in the UK', Final report to the DETR, November 2000, pp. 213-215. On SAGE, see M. Mitchell Waldrop, 'The Origins of Personal Computing' in Scientific American, Vol. 285. No. 6, December 2001.

13 D. C. Mowery and R. Rosenberg, 'Technical Change in the Commercial Aircraft Industry, 1925-75' in R Rosenberg, 'Inside the Black Box: Technology and Economics', Cambridge University Press, 1982.

14 The most realistic historical analysis is in Frederick C. Thayer, 'Airline Regulation: The Case for a 'Public Utility Approach', Logistics and Transportation Review, September 1982.

15 'New' Labour's knowledge of these matters may be judged by the remark of a former Cabinet Minister, a leading architect of the Blair 'Project', who told us that 'Labour should never have nationalised British Airways!' The facts are in Higham, op. cit., and Davies, E. '"National" Capitalism', Gollancz, London, 1939, Ch. XII.

16 William M. Burden, 'The Future of Air Transport: An American View', in (ed) Lord Brabazon of Tara, 'Air Transport and Civil Aviation, 1944-5', Todd, London and New York,

17 For the origins of the bilateral system see 'British Air Transport in the Seventies: Report of the Committee of Inquiry into Civil Air Transport', (the 'Edwards Committee'), Cmnd 4018, HMSO, London, May, 1969, pp 2-5. Appendices 3 to 6 provide basic data on international organisations in air transport, the content of some important bilateral agreements, and definitions of the Freedoms of the Air.

18 The European Commission has now renewed the exemption of IATA tariff conferences from EU Competition rules, ATW On-line, 26 June 2002, www.atonline.com

19 Professor Kahn described this phase at CAB at the New York Society of Security Analysts, 2 February 1978.

20 In a typical year, the CAA might have frozen certain fares to about thirty countries which, under its 'key routes' approach, would affect many more. See, for example the CAA Annual Report, 1985-6, p. 12. The effect is shown by CAA's analysis of the situation before the current EU

regime came into existence: 'International scheduled fares for on-demand passengers from the UK are the lowest in the Community on a rate per km. basis, with fares from most other Member states being at least 30 per cent higher than UK levels ... ex-UK full fares are roughly the same as their equivalents in the US domestic market.' CAA, 'Airline Competition in the Single European Market, CAP 623, London November 1993.

21 Richard O'Melia quoted in Paul Stephen Dempsey and Andrew R. Goetz, 'Airline Deregulation and Laissez Faire Mythology', Quorum, Westport and London, 1992.

22 This was called 'Safety by Objectives' – an extreme form of the voluntary Code of Conduct approach. It was dropped so quickly that there are few public references. See P. W. Reed, 'Romance and Reality', Presidential Address to Transport Studies Association. 1983.

23 Quoted in Dempsey and Goetz, op.cit., page 223.

24 We write from direct experience, having been subjected to many hours of intensive re-education by the economists who spearheaded US deregulation.

25 Edmund Greenslet: 'World Airline Capital Requirements', Chicago Convention 50th. Anniversary Conference, October 1994.) Quoted by Paul Stephen Dempsey and Laurence E. Gesell, in their 'Airline Management for the 21st Century', CoastAir, Chandler, Arizona, 2001, page 310. They conclude that 'airline prices have fallen at a much slower rate since deregulation than before it.'

26 The Bureau of Labour Statistics figures are widely used in US official policy making, e.g. in Nancy Kelly's 'Comments on Market Power' for the Legislative Task Force of the Utah Public Services Commission, 8 September 1998.

27 CAA, 'Traffic distribution policy and airport and airspace capacity over the next 15 years', CAP 570, July 1990, para 6, page A1/4. This is the accepted view in the industry, as reflected in Thomas J. Gallagher, 'Aircraft Finance and Airline Financial Analysis in the Fifth Cycle Of The Jet Age', in (ed) Darryl Jenkins and Cecilia Preble Ray, 'Handbook of Airline Economics', McGraw Hill, Falls Church, VA, 1995, pp. 227-8. The government also record this obvious truth, which sits uneasily with its theological devotion to 'liberalisation', in CDATP, Chapter 2, para. 42.

28 For a crushing demolition of the bizarre claims put forward on behalf of US deregulation, e.g. by the Brookings Institute, see Dempsey and Gesell, page 312-315.

29 I am indebted to Mel Brenner for this point. Mr. Brenner was Vice President Market Planning for both American Airlines and Trans World Airlines, and also held a number of senior US official posts.

30 A detailed account of this process is by A M Milne and A Laing, 'The Obligation To Carry', Institute of Transport, London, 1956.

31 A. Goetz, quoted in Dempsey and Gesell, op.cit., pp. 427-8.

32 Dempsey and Gesell, op. cit., page 291-301.

33 The publicly owned British Airways pioneered the scientific analysis of fare types, leading to such revolutionary concepts as APEX fares, as shown in the (then) Overseas Division paper 'Segmental Seat Scheduling', January 1974.

34 W. David Slawson, 'The New Inflation: The Collapse of Free Markets', Princeton University Press, Princeton and Guildford, 1981, p 51.

35 Julius Maldutis, 'The Airlines: $99 Forever', Salomon Brothers Inc., April 1983. This is a classic analysis by one of Wall Street's most acute observers.

36 The quality data are from the Zagat Airline Survey, 1990-5, quoted in Dempsey and Goetz, pp. 274-5, and the aircraft fleet age information, ibid. p 222-3.

37 Air Transport World, 13 February, 2001. In an attempt to neutralise a passenger bill of rights being proposed in the US Congress, airlines have incorporated 'customer service commitments' into contracts of carriage.

38 Ralph Nader, 'Squeezing Coach Class', The Nader Page (Internet), 8 February 1999. The Aviation Consumer Action Project points out (16 August 2000) that the huge delays – with one in four flights more than a hour late – are the result of airline scheduling practices, i.e. 'hubbing'. See www.acap1971.org

39 Although now factually dated, the classic analyses are still M. A. Brenner, J. O. Leet, and E. Schott, 'Airline Deregulation', Eno Foundation, Westport, Conn., 1985; and Airline Economics Inc., 'Airline Consolidation – Where it stands – what's to come', Washington D.C., 1987.

40 Described in Richard J. Fahy, Jr., 'The Cutting Edge Of Technology And Regulation' in (ed) C F Butler and M R Keller, 'Handbook Of Airline Marketing', Chapter 53, McGraw Hill, 1995.

41 This is now a classic business case study. See Robert G. Cross 'Revenue Management', Broadway Books, New York, 1997, Chapter 4, 'The Attack of the Laser fares.'. Professor Kahn's view of the matter can be found in his 'Macroeconomic Consequences ...' op. cit.

42 These issues are well discussed in Doug Henwood. 'Wall Street', Verso, London and New York, 1998, Chapter 6, Governance.
43 Peter Rona, IBJ Schroder Bank and Trust, New York, 1989, quoted by Henwood, page 272.
44 Dempsey and Goetz, op. cit., Chapter 2, 'Corporate Pirates and Robber Barons in the Cockpit.'
45 Ibid., pp 29-32.
46 At United, baggage drivers used to waste scarce apron time weaving around ground equipment to check aircraft numbers which were then painted on the noses. The former management wouldn't listen to its employees. In the new, improved atmosphere, United agreed to stencil numbers on the sides of aircraft fuselages. This had a significant impact on apron productivity.
47 Economic Policy Institute, 'The State Of Working America', 1994-5, Washington DC. This is a biennial publication and a comprehensive source on US wages prices and living standards. The 2000-1 edition reports 'After more than 15 years of stagnation and decline, inflation-adjusted wages began to rise in 1995', See Executive Summary www.epinet.org.books/swa
48 Robert Brenner, 'The Boom and the Bubble: the US in the World Economy', Verso, London and New York, 2002, is a convincing recent analysis of this process. An incisive treatment from a different perspective is that of Frederick C. Thayer, 'Rebuilding America: The Case for Economic Regulation', Praeger, New York, 1984, Chapter 2.
49 This is known as the 'S-curve'. Dempsey and Gesell give credit to William Fruhan. 'The Fight for Competitive Advantage', 1972. But it is fair to say that the industry had long been aware of this effect.
50 This term dates from the South Sea Bubble when worthless shares were sold by the bucket.
51 This 'yield erosion' is happening on a global scale, as illustrated by Uli Baur in 'Winning Strategies in a Changing Global Environment' in the (ed.) Gail F. Butler and Martin R. Keller, 'Handbook of Airline Marketing', op. cit.1998, page 540.
52 Robert L Crandall, 'The Unique US Airline Industry', in the (ed.) Darryl Jenkins and Cecilia Preble Day, 'Handbook of Airline Economics', op. cit., pp. 3-12.
53 Dempsey and Gesell, op. cit., Chapter 3, 'Airline Finance'.
54 Dempsey and Gesell point out that, by the mid-nineties, the American airlines had debt totalling $35 billion or 'more than eight times the industry's total accumulated profit from the beginning of commercial aviation until 1988.' Ibid. p 97. The US Federal Government has announced a $10-15 billion aid programme for the US airlines, claiming that this is necessitated by the after effects of the New York terrorist attacks.
55 Dempsey and Gesell, ibid. p 138 ff. The Standard and Poor's Debt Ratings are quoted on p. 149.
56 Philip Baggaley of Standard and Poor's, quoted in Dempsey and Gesell, ibid. p 146
57 Dempsey and Gesell, ibid., p. 162 quote a European Community report that, during the 1970s and 1980s, the US government gave its airline industry between $33.5 and $41.5 billion in direct and indirect support. In addition, tax deferrals and exemptions have exceeded $3.5 billions since 1976.
58 Robert W. Mann, Jr., Vice President SH &E, 'US Airline Issues and the State of American Airlines' presentation to Wings Club, New York, 13 September, 1993. This compares the two Dallas based companies, American and Southwest.
59 We were sceptical until we spent time with the company, its employees and trade union officials. The (genuinely) co-operative atmosphere at Southwest is the most extraordinary – and successful! – we have ever encountered. It also has eccentric features such as a President who sometimes appears in drag.
60 The Wright Amendment restricts operations at Dallas Love Field to states contiguous to Texas. That rules out many of the MegaCarriers' direct services to e.g. Chicago and New York .
61 Morten, Beyer and Agnew 'What Is Really Wrong With America's Air Carriers or The Secret of Southwest Airlines', Washington and London, August 1998 .
62 It is almost impossible to keep up with the Ansett saga, given the number of efforts to revive it. The Australian government was so eager to see its re-emergence that it guaranteed slots at Sydney together with 'fast track safety approval'. ATW-online, 29 November, 2001.
63 ATW-online 4 December, 2001.
64 CAA, 'Airline Competition in the European Single Market', CAP 623, November 1993, pp 19-21. Everything that has since happened in Australia and Canada since this date confirmed the CAA's judgement that the 'prospects for significant new entry ... appear doubtful', para 82.
65 This was a key driving force behind the CAA's interventionist policy in the nineteen seventies. Until recently, action was still being taken against certain 'on-demand' tariffs.
66 European Commission communication, 'The European Airline Industry: from Single Market To World-Wide Challenges', Brussels, 1999, page 18.

67 Karel van Miert, EU Competition Commissioner in Brussels Aviation Report, Beaumont and Sons, London, February 1999. As for the new airline Alliances leading to 'fierce competition', Van Miert has noted 'evidence to the contrary.' Interestingly, he also suggests that the 'old interlining system' gave passengers wider opportunities for access to services than the 'more closed' system of alliances.

68 We can't check this point but recall from memory that tariff freedom for small operators (against their opposition!) was negotiated in the ECAC/INFA committee, long before the EU had a role. Moreover, there were a thousand plus unused routes under the (then) existing 'restrictive' bilateral agreements, mainly for the 'secondary' airports which are favoured by the low cost operators.

69 Thayer, Logistics and Transport Review, op. cit.

70 European Council Regulation (EEC) no. 95/93.

71 A revised Slots Regulation has still not appeared: the European MegaCarriers ferociously oppose any abolition of Grandfather Rights. The current proposals are therefore of a tidying up nature, but there is promise of something 'more radical' to come.

72 This practice requires an Exemption from Competition Law.

73 CAA, 'Slot Allocation: A Proposal For Europe's Airports', CAP 644, London, February 1995, para 103.

74 CAA, ibid., para 110.

75 Letter from Director General of Fair Trading to Secretary of State for Trade and Industry, 31 July 1998, para 22, circulated with DTI Press Release on 'BA/A Alliance – Consultation on DGFT's Advice', 6 August 1998.

76 OFT, op. cit, para 24.

77 John Hulet, Hugh Lake and Graham Perry, 'Study on Airport Slot Allocation', Final Report commissioned by UK Department of Transport, SD Scicon UK Ltd., Camberley, 1991.

78 Tokyo slot restrictions prevented the two British airlines mounting the frequencies they were allowed under the UK/Japan air services agreement. As with the former Dan Air slots at Gatwick, a licensing hearing proved to be an ideal way of settling the issue.

79 This was established in internal CAA research some thirty years ago.

80 Peter Villa, former Managing Director of Air UK mentioned in Skyport (quoted in ABTN, 3 April, 2001), nine or ten regional airports which have lost their Heathrow services. If short haul routes to European destinations were added, the tally would be much higher.

81 OFT op. cit. para 22.

82 As CAA point out, 'providing extra capacity at regional airports would not be an effective substitute of additional capacity in the south east'. See 'Traffic Distribution Policy and Airspace Capacity: the next 15 years', CAP 570, July 1990. Conclusions like this are based on elaborate modelling studies.

83 The basic principle was to split 'heavy' routes and transfer some of their traffic from Heathrow to Gatwick, and to transfer the entire traffic of 'thin' routes with low interlining content.

84 This was announced in the consultation document, CDTAP, para 220.

85 CAA, 'Competitive Provision of Infrastructure and Services Within Airports', Consultation paper, February 2001.

86 BAA Annual Report and Accounts, 2000-01.

87 Andrew Wileman and Michael Jary, 'Retail Power Plays: From Trading to Brand Leadership', Macmillan Business, Basingstoke and London, 1997, page 77.

88 Ibid. The marketing term for this is 'proximity retailing.'

89 British Airways, 'The Future of Aviation', April 2001, page 18 refers to the failure to 'maintain quality standards', which also includes non-runway congestion.

90 The Air Transport Users' Council's remit has never extended to BAA airports. The Council is based at the CAA and has often been seen, rather unfairly, as being in the pocket of that body.

91 CTDAP, para 37.

92 CTDAP, para 42.

93 These battles have long raged behind the scenes. Now the press has noticed, e.g. in 'Airports fail to deliver: operator accused of promoting shopping while passengers suffer' in The Guardian, 6 June 2002.

94 Civil Aviation Authority, 'Traffic Distribution Policy and Airspace and Airport Capacity: the Next 15 Years', op. cit. and Civil Aviation Authority, 'Traffic Distribution Policy for the London Area and Strategic Options for the Longer Term', CAP 548, 1989.

95 BAA plc, 'Traffic Distribution … Longer Term', Comments, April 1989.

96 British Airways emphasise this in 'The Future of Aviation' April 2001, page 10.

97 Peter Berdy, 'Developing Effective Route Networks', Chapter 47, Handbook of Airline Marketing, op. cit.
98 Arthur D. Little, op. cit., page 19.
99 British Airways op. cit. refer to 'an intensifying airport capacity crisis in south east England', page 17. BA add that 'an assumption that current policies have resulted in UK airports meeting the needs of users while keeping costs low ... is a serious misconception.'
100 CAA, 'Heathrow, Gatwick, Stansted and Manchester Airports Price Caps, 2003-2008', CAA Summary and Preliminary Conclusions, November 2001. This is a highly complex exercise in scholastic logic, and we can only deal with the main themes here
101 Ibid., page 13.
102 Ibid., page 10.
103 Ibid., pp. 10-11 were CAA admits that 'a full move to market clearing prices ... would create perverse incentives.'
104 Ibid., page 23.
105 Ibid., page 4.
106 Ibid., page 14.
107 Ibid., page 21.
108 As we write, the Competition Commission has issued an interim statement on the CAA's 'dual till' proposals, basically agreeing with our own arguments, apart from the strange conclusion that 'there is no evidence that the single till has led to under-investment', Statement of 11 July, 2002.
109 According to Oxford Economic Forecasting, 'The Contribution of the Aviation Industry to the UK Economy', November 1999, aviation contributes more than £10 billion a year to UK GDP and, directly and indirectly, generates more than half a million jobs.
110 This was 275,000 air transport movements per annum. The current Heathrow figure is now probably approaching 400, 000 per annum! See CDTAP, op. cit., Chapter Two, para 39.
111 Thayer, 'Rebuilding America', op. cit. page 82. Professor Thayer was a US Air Force logistics expert, and thus has an especially acute eye for the wastes of competition.
112 CAA , 'Heathrow, Gatwick ... Price Caps, 2003-2008', page 9.
113 DETR, 'Guidance on Methodologies for Airports in the South East and Eastern Region of England', 2000 sets out the appraisal framework, November 2000, 5.1.
114 Commission on the Third London Airport ('the Roskill report'), Report, HMSO, London, January 1971.
115 Nathaniel Lichfield, 'Community Impact Evaluation' UCL Press, London, 1996 is a lucid exposition by one of the world's leading practitioners.
116 The definitive critique is in the papers of the Labour Finance and Industry Group seminar, 'Transport As If People Mattered', held at the Royal Town Planning Institute, June 2000, chaired by the present writer, with contributions by Ashis Choudhury, Nathaniel Lichfield and Alan Wenban-Smith.
117 DETR, 'Appraisal Framework for Airports in the South East and Eastern regions of England: A Consultation Paper.', Part B, para 6.2.
118 CDTAP Consultation Paper, Chapter Six, para 131.
119 CDTAP Consultation Paper, Appendix 'Valuing the External Costs of Aviation'.
120 Ibid. para 5.
121 Ibid. para 8.
122 The Batho Committee. See the Royal Commission on Environmental Pollution, 'Transport and the Environment', Cmnd 2674, HMSO, London, 1994, para 7.76.
123 Information on Manchester Airport can be found at www.manairport.co.uk
124 CAA, 'Connecting Traffic at UK Airports', May 1998.
125 CDTAP, op. cit. para 200.
126 British Airways, op. cit., page 17.
127 Leading experts in this field are discussing various ways that the public can share in 'planning gain', not excluding the ideas of Henry George. See Nathaniel Lichfield and Owen Connellan, 'Land Value and Community Betterment Taxation in Britain: Proposals for Legislation and Practice', Lincoln Institute of Land policy Working paper, 2000.
128 IPECAC Documents can be downloaded from www.ipcc.ch
129 US National Academy of Sciences, 'Climate Change Science: An Analysis of Some Key Questions', Washington DC, June 2001. See John Bellamy Foster, 'Ecology Against Capitalism' for an informative discussion on this, in Monthly Review, Vol. 53. No.5, October 2001.
130 National Academies National Research Council, 'Abrupt Climate Change', National Academies Press, Washington DC, 2001, Executive Summary, opening para.

131 Ibid., page 2.
132 CDTAP op. cit. quotes the IPCC report to the effect that, of the human contributions to climate change, aviation is responsible for 3.5 per cent, Chapter Six, para 129.
133 DETR says, op. cit. para 131, that the government 'is particularly keen to develop the use of economic instruments'. The figures are from 'Valuing the External Costs of Aviation', paras 22-24.
134 William D. Nordhaus and Joseph Boyer, 'Roll the DICE Again: The Economics of Global Warming', October 1999, Summary, Major Results. Page 4. The full study was published under this title by Yale University Press, same date. Professor Nordhaus has written numerous papers on the same theme. See his web site www.econ.yale.edu/~nordhaus/homepage
135 Robert Constanza, Review of 'Managing the commons: the economics of climate change', 1994 by William D Nordhaus, to appear in 'Environmental Science and Technology.' Web site.
136 C. Perrings, K. G. Malern, C. Folke, C. S. Holling and B-O Jansson, 'Biodiversity Loss: Economic and Ecological Issues', Cambridge University Press, 1995.
137 The US House of Representatives passed legislation to ban Concorde as a retaliatory measure. See Environment News Service, March 3, 1999.
138 This was done by agreeing, in ICAO, to the American approach which renders effective action far more difficult. The President of the European Commission responded to this knock out by declaring 'a victory for Europe because the US will withdraw their complaint and the threat of economic sanctions.' Brussels Aviation Report, November 2001.
139 Royal Commission, op. cit., para 5.40.
140 CAA, 'National Air Traffic Services: Setting the Charge Conditions for the North Atlantic Service Provided by NATS for the First Five Years', June 2000, para 2.3 suggests that there is 'at least some potential contestability', i.e. a possibility that 'ICAO could reallocate the right to provide the service to another state'.
141 DETR, 'A Public Private Partnership For National Air Traffic Services Ltd. (NATS)', October 1998.
142 Minutes of DETR Committee Meeting with 'NATS Stakeholders', 7 December, 1999, para 6.
143 These proposals are explained in DETR 'Consultation on ... "the Creation of the Single European Sky"', which reprints the European Commission document, COM(1999) 614 Brussels, 1 December 1999.
144 House of Commons ETRA Sub-committee on National Air Traffic Services, evidence by Tony Goldman (DETR), questions 114-117, Wed 19 November 1998.
145 Readers wouldn't believe our most amusing experiences, so we confine ourselves to the following. When out of their depth, high level private sector appointees tend to dwell on what is familiar to them: they review head office fire regulations, make rulings on who can use the Board Room or, as on one memorable occasion, write by hand a red ink memo about 'Disposal of Kitchen Waste'.
146 Gordon Brown, Robin Cook and John Prescott, 'Financing Infrastructure Development: Promoting a Partnership Between Public and Private Finance', Labour Finance and Industry Group Symposium, February 1994.
147 The present writer's paper for Clare Short's policy conference, 'Transport Policy For Britain – Finance For Transport', January 1996, reflects the prevailing view of the time that a Labour Chancellor would be '*obliged* to look at alternative sources to *supplement*' public investment funds.
148 The 1996 paper emphasised that public sector objectives should be dominant, and that only certain risks should be transferred to the private sector, e.g. for cost overruns. After ridiculing the Treasury's PSBR definition, it argued that the public sector should be able to approach capital markets directly. It also highlighted the perverse effects of targetry, using prisons as an example. No one foresaw that a future Labour government would set itself a target for 'prison assaults' ... and fail to meet it! In the event, few if any risks are being transferred to the private sector under Labour's PFI/PPP approach.
149 British Airways, 'Financing the Future', 28 October 1979. Of the other 80 per cent, it was in retained earnings or commercial loans, mostly negotiated in foreign markets with a Treasury Guarantee.
150 The present writer's brief for John Prescott, 'PSBR and All That – the Only Treasury In Step?', March 1992 was a basis for this campaign. Ironically, 'New' Labour has retained the silliest of the Treasury's Flexible Dogmas!
151 Pliatzky, Sir Leo, 'Getting and Spending: Public Expenditure, Employment and Inflation', Blackwell, Oxford, 1982.

152 Ibid. page 192.
153 Our 'Transport Policy ... Finance for Transport', op. cit., pointed out the defects of this approach for NATS, together with other examples such as rolling stock leasing for the LU Northern Line – lessons rapidly forgotten when Labour took office!
154 The new En Route Centre at Swanwick missed practically every milestone from 1995, and the private sector contractors had their contract terminated prematurely. Hardly an argument for an even bigger role for the private sector.
155 Industry itself is very sceptical about this. Computer Weekly 'has repeatedly expressed concern that, by handing over the intellectual property rights to systems built under the PFI, the Government creates the impression that a faulty supplier can never be kicked off a PFI computing project', in 'Counting the Cost', 5 April 2001.
156 Loss of technical interoperability due to marketisation can create huge problems, as with the major airport (not in Britain) which has three computer systems, none of which can talk to each other.
157 There is a widespread impression that NATS is in legal form a non-profit company, but this is not true. Its Memorandum of Association allows NATS to 'carry on business as a general commercial company and to carry out any trade or business whatever.'
158 This was made by a junior DETR Minister, Robert Ainsworth, in the Fourth Standing Committee on Delegated Legislation, 12 February 2001.
159 DETR, 'A Public Private Partnership for National Air Traffic Services Ltd. (NATS): A Report on the Response to the Public Consultation ...', July 1999, para 16.
160 The Response document is no more than a series of assertions. For example, there is no attempt to justify the proposition that it is a good thing to 'incentivise' private sector Air Traffic Service providers to 'make and retain a profit.
161 See the BALPA 'Response ... on a Public/Private Partnership for National Air Traffic Services Ltd. (NATS)', January 1999, available at www.balpa.org. As we write, a BALPA press release of 30 July 2002, referring to a report just published by the House of Commons Transport Select Committee, says BALPA 'shares the Committee's unease at NATS' reductions in the number of its safety critical staff.'
162 The Canadian, German and New Zealand Air Traffic models of organisation are rejected, but no evidence is offered for this conclusion. As usual, the argument is entirely theological. Ibid. para 18.
163 Roger Ford, 'WCRM finally collapses – sort-of – official', Modern Railways, December 2001.
164 Arthur D Little's 'Study ...' op. cit. highlights this conflict of interest, noting the 'emphasis by NATS on increased airport capacity as opposed to efficiency improvements, which are likely to benefit airlines much more, through reduced costs, than they will benefit NATS', page 6.
165 Most professional sources are difficult for lay readers. P. W. Reed, 'The Economics of Public Enterprise', Butterworth, London, 1972, Chapter 2, Investment Decision Making, includes worked examples illustrating the various concepts, and the effect of different criteria and discount rates.
166 Roger Ford, 'Signalling investment crisis deepens ... Could there be something wrong with the business rather than the signalling?', Modern Railways, July 1999.
167 See consultants' calculations enclosed with DETR News Release of 8 December 1999, 'PPP Is The Best Option For London's Underground'. This is clearly heading in the Railtrack direction. See Roger Ford, 'Railtrack investment- – money into a black hole', Modern Railways, July 2001.
168 The situation as summed up by the transport industry's professional body, CIT World: 'Broken rails: 'Railtrack significantly worse'', 03, February 2001.
169 Richard Middleton, 'An Engineering Strategy for Railtrack', Modern Railways, March 2002.
170 Roger Ford, 'WCRM finally collapses ...'. [West Coast Route Modernisation.] The 'gauge corner cracking' which played a role in the Hatfield disaster is not merely the result of faulty track maintenance but also of poorly maintained vehicles. See Roger Ford, 'Gauge corner cracking – privatisation indicted', Modern Railways, January 2002.
171 It is not too much to say that this was the main theme of 'New' Labour's media 'spin' campaign on London Underground infrastructure privatisation.
172 Down from a peak of 58,000 in 1979.
173 This is based on a detailed study we undertook for John Prescott, 'British Airways Over The Last Two Decades', December 1993. Ministers are thus fully aware of the true facts.
174 Avmark Inc., 'The Competitiveness of the European Community's Air Transport Industry', prepared for the European Commission, 28 February, 1992, para 3.4.2.

175 Ibid., para 5.4.
176 Ibid., para 5.9,.
177 Allyson Pollock, Jean Shaoul and Neil Vickers, 'Private Finance and 'value for money' in NHS hospitals: a policy in search of a rationale?', British Medical Journal, 2002;324:1205-1209, 18 May 2002, deal lucidly with this, and other relevant points. The editorial in the same issue of BMJ is entitled 'Myopia and the private finance initiative'.
178 Nathaniel Lichfield, 'Economics in urban conservation', Cambridge University Press, 1988, page 246. Professor Lichfield gives a lucid example of how the discounting technique is applied.
179 Ibid. page 247. I am indebted to Professor Lichfield for help on this, and much else, over the years.
180 This is now even admitted in circles friendly to 'New' Labour, for example in the Institute of Public Policy Research report on Public-Private Partnerships of June 2001.
181 According to Maurice Fitzpatrick of Chantrey Vellacott DFK (described by Lord MacDonald, then Minister of Transport, as 'one of the UK's top accountancy firms'), the 'Treasury could easily incur additional capital expenditure of upwards £40 billion [by direct borrowing] during the next five years … and still keep within the present rules.' Mr. Fitzpatrick's briefing of 12 May 1999, 'Tube Fares Will Have To Be Some 30% Higher As A Result Of The Planned £7 billion Public Private Partnership …'
182 Airline pilots' experience suggests that, where NATS did provide such facilities, they were of an excellent standard. As we write, a Report from the House of Commons Transport, Local Government and Regions Committee is saying that NATS' 'reduction in engineering staff seems misplaced', and that it is 'not convinced that NATS' systems are sufficiently robust to enable it to reduce the numbers of safety critical staff'. Eighteenth Report, Conclusions and Recommendations, (h) and (i), 17 June 2002.
183 House of Commons Environment, Transport and Regional Affairs Committee, 'Aviation Safety', HC 275, 21 July 1999.
184 Memorandum to House of Commons ETRA Committee on 'Aviation Safety' from the British Air Line Pilots' Association, para 6.4.
185 The writer speaks from much personal experience. The argument about splitting organisations leading to 'greater transparency' is truly nonsensical.
186 J. M. Ramsden, 'The Safe Airline', MacDonald and Jane's, London 1976, page 185. This is a brilliantly realistic analysis which deserves to be read in full.
187 ETRA Committee, BALPA, op. cit., para 6.5.
188 This concept was put forward by the airline consortium at a meeting of the DETR Parliamentary Labour Party (back bench) Committee with 'NATS Stakeholders' on 7 December 1999, at which the present writer also voiced the opposition to privatisation of the LFIG Transport Study Group.
189 Jean Shaoul, 'Debt model fails to take off', Public Finance, December 2001.
190 Adam Smith in 'The Wealth of Nations', p 573, Book V – of the Revenue of the Sovereign or Commonwealth, Chapter I – Of the Expenses of the Sovereign or Commonwealth, Part III – of the expenses of public Works and public Institutions, Article I – of the public Works and Institutions for facilitating the commerce of society.
191 In most countries, government agencies provide lighthouses. In Britain, a charitable body, Trinity House, is responsible under a Royal Charter. Private lights were abolished in 1836.
192 'British Air Transport in the Seventies: Report of the Committee of Inquiry into Civil Air Transport', (the 'Edwards Report'), HMSO, Cmnd 4018, May 1969.
193 Guardian Unlimited, 'Hewitt admits Labour's industry errors', May 16 2002, reported the Secretary of State for Industry's admission that, since 1995, French and German manufacturing output had risen 20% while UK output had largely bumped along, and that French manufacturing productivity was 32% higher and Germany 29% higher than in Britain. http://guardian.co.uk
194 Colin Crouch, 'The Future of Employment in Western Europe', Sussex European Institute Working Paper no. 4, 1994, page 5.
195 N. F. Simpson, 'One Way Pendulum', a 'Farce in a New Dimension', Faber, London, 1960.
196 R. M. Cotterill, Director Economic Policy and Regulation, CAA, 'Open Skies, Competition and Regulation', 18 January 1999.
197 Air Services Agreement between the Government of the United Kingdom of Great Britain and Northern Ireland and the Government of the United States of America, 'Bermuda II', signed 23 July, 1977, Consolidated Version DETR, June 2001.

198 For example, the UK and US governments are now reported to have agreed additional services which will allow British Midland and certain US carriers to mount operations from Heathrow.

199 The CAA aimed to prevent this happening, just as much as to stop certain travellers being exploited. This is the rationale of the classical 'cost related' tariffs policy.

200 The graph is from Roberts, Roach and Associates Inc., 'Economic Benefits of Open Skies', Hayward, CA, who give permission to reproduce with attribution. British Airways publish a graph showing a marked fall in international fares since 1970 in 'The Future of Aviation', op. cit., page 2.

201 The 1978 version of 'UK Route 1: Scheduled Combination Air Service' gave the UK 13 US Gateway points, two of them deferred for three years, with no intermediate points. The 2001 version gave the UK 21 points, with the possibility of intermediate points in seven European countries. 'Bermuda II', Annex One, Route Schedules.

202 In airline jargon, these are 'Negative Add-ons'.

203 Third and Fourth Freedoms are the ability for states to carry traffic from State A to State B, and from State B to State A. Fifth Freedom rights are where airlines from Country A can carry traffic between Countries B and C.

204 Air Services Agreements may include Confidential Memoranda of Understanding (CMUs). Country A may want 'Open Skies', whereas Country B may be strongly opposed. A solution might be a published treaty stressing 'free competition', while an annex or 'side letter', hidden from public view, contains 'safeguards', acceptable to Country B.

205 Robert Ayling (then) Chief Executive revealed that British Airways' real aim was a full merger with American Airlines in his Beaumont Lecture to the Royal Aeronautical Society, 13 October 1998, Brussels Aviation Report, November 1998.

206 Most recently, a US federal judge dismissed claims by Virgin Atlantic that British Airways has a monopoly on certain routes between Heathrow and the USA on the grounds that Virgin did not provide sufficient evidence. The American law courts are well on the way to comprehensive regulation of British airlines. Brussels Aviation Report, Beaumont and Sons, November 1999.

207 This is a crucially important point. If not embodied in a formal air services treaty, the Americans may record the point in a unilateral 'side letter'.

208 Van Miert, op. cit. He also makes the highly significant admission that it is by no means clear that existing 'remedies' are sufficient to deal with 'anti-competitive effects' of the Alliances.

209 Paul Stephen Dempsey, 'Globalisation as a Euphemism for Cartellisation', Handbook of Airline Marketing, op. cit., Chapter 34.

210 These are BA and BMA. Unlike them, Virgin is not in a major Alliance and opposes the US 'Open Skies' proposals.

211 Roberts Roach & Associates, for American Airlines, 'Economic Benefits of US-UK Open Skies', Hayward, California, CA, October 1996, Appendix A

212 Loyola de Palacio, Vice-president of the European Commission, 'Globalisation: The Way Forward', Speech to IATA World Air Transport Summit, Madrid, 28 May 2001.

213 'External competence' would give the European Commission power to approve, or even negotiate, air services agreements between individual member states and third non-EU-member countries.

214 One of Blair's Spanish allies, de Palacio, see (212), is an extreme proponent of deregulation.

215 R. M. Cotterill, op. cit., paras 29-30.

216 Sir Malcolm Field, CAA Chairman has also urged the creation of a 'single and competitive global aviation market' in Transport Review, 1999.

217 According to the CAA, code sharing is 'not needed to co-ordinate schedules, to ensure that baggage is transferred reliably and quickly, to have cross membership of frequent flyer programmes, to arrange for connecting flights to use connecting gates at the same terminal' etc. CAA, 'Airline Competition on European Long Haul Routes', CAP 639, 1994, para 234, page 57.

218 CAA Official Record, Series 2, No. 1388, Part 4, Tariff Filings in the UK under Council Regulation (EEC) No. 2409/92.

219 European Commission aviation officials are guarded in what they say in public, but the argument has been forcefully made to the present writer. More than once! Certain operators are pushing the present EU rules on 'wet leasing' to the limit, and the Blair government appears to approve of this.

220 Willem de Ruiter, 'European Shipping head slams lax safety regime' in CILT World (Chartered Institute of Logistics and Transport), 05, January 2002.

221 Quoted in CILT World, ibid., page 10.

222 John Lang, quoted in CILT World, ibid.

223 William Greider, 'The Right and US Trade Law: Invalidating the 20th. Century', The Nation, 15 October, 2001, is informative on takings theory. See www.thenation.com Robert Kuttner, 'Everything for Sale: the Virtues and Limits of Markets', University of Chicago Press, Chicago 1999 is informative on the Law and Economics school, and is an excellent general survey of developments in the USA, including airline deregulation.

224 Mary Bottari, 'NAFTA's Investor "Rights", A Corporate Dream, A Citizen Nightmare' in Multinational Monitor, Vol. 22, No. 3, April 2001, pp. 7-8. See www.essential.org

225 Bottari ibid., page 8.

226 Bottari, ibid., page 2.

227 Bottari, ibid. pp. 3-4. The implications are graphically portrayed in a headline in the Canadian news magazine, Report: 'Is Canada Post illegal? A little known NAFTA clause threatens (or promises) the end of government intervention?', 2 April 2001.

228 Greider, op. cit. pp.-3

229 Jeff Faux, 'A Deal Built on Sand', The American Prospect, Special Supplement, Winter 2002, is an excellent analysis of current TO negotiations. His 'Rethinking the Global Political Economy', speech to Asia-Europe-US Progressive Scholars' Forum, Japan, 11-15 April, 2002, is a constructive survey of the issues. Available on www.epinet.org

230 For example, 'Gordon Brown embraces market forces', The Guardian, 29 March 2002.

231 Colin Crouch and Wolfgang Streeck, 'Political Economy of Modern Capitalism', Sage, London, 1997. This is essential reading for any serious student of globalisation.

232 European Commission officials have explained how they would approach the issue. See summary of evidence by Ben van Houtte (DGVII) to House of Lords European Communities Committee in Brussels Aviation Report, London, January 1999. For the technicalities, see CAA, 'Airline Competition on European Long Haul Routes', CAP 639, November 1994, para 162.

233 The rationale is set out in CAA, 'European Air Fares – a discussion document', CAP 409, London 1977, which contains original research, some of it done jointly with airlines. The document has no modern counterpart: contemporary publications tend to be exercises in applied theology.

234 'European Air Fares ...', ibid. Appendix 7.

235 Gregory, Martyn, 'Dirty Tricks, British Airways' secret war against Virgin Atlantic', Little Brown, London, 1994.

236 In its heyday, the CAA also performed the functions of the Competition Commission and the Office of Fair Trading, with the latter bodies reluctant to get involved in such a technical area.

237 Prescott, John, 'Labour's Aviation Policy', presented to a conference of the aviation trade unions at Bishops Stortford in 1990 or 1991.

238 As demonstrated later, even Mrs. Thatcher accepted this approach to air transport.

239 John Prescott, op. cit.

240 By 'operational', we mean giving official policy makers, administrators or regulators some broad idea of what to do. For example, it is difficult to read any meaning whatever into terms like 'reform'.

241 Ronald Englefield, 'The Critique of Pure Verbiage: Essays on Abuses of Language in Literary, Religious and Philosophical Writings', Open Court, La Salle, Ill., 1990

242 Dick Morris, 'Behind the Oval Office', Random House, New York, 1997, and 'The New Prince', Renaissance Books, Los Angeles, 1999.

243 Morris (1997), ibid., pp. 60-1.

244 Morris (1997), ibid., Chapter Five, 'Triangulation'.

245 Morris (1997), ibid. pp. 236-7 on 'lifestyle groups'. Apparently hikers, campers, people who love technology and baseball fans are 'swing voters.'

246 Morris (1999), op. cit., Chapter Seven, 'Transcending the Architecture of Parties'.

247 Morris (1997), op. cit. pp. 37-8. Item Five in a list which sums up just about the entire content of 'New' Labour.

248 George Stephanopoulos, 'All Too Human', Little Brown, Boston, New York, London, 1999, p 382. Perhaps the best source for understanding 'New' Democrat/'New' Labour thinking.

249 The remarkable continuity at the Ministry of Transport is illustrated by Professor C. D. Foster who was recruited by Mrs. Castle but still played a major role in devising the structure of privatised railways.

250 The best features in Labour's 1968 Transport Act, like Passenger Transport Authorities, were successful because they drew upon Labour's own experience of problems in conurbations.

251 Ministry of Transport, 'Road Pricing: the Economic and Technical Possibilities', ('the Smeed Report'), HMSO, London, 1964.

252 FitzRoy and Smith, 'Priority over Pricing: Lessons from Zurich on the Redundancy of Road Pricing', Journal of Transport Economics and Policy, May 1993. Zurich, with its strong environmental aims, and 'reserved tracks' with traffic light priorities for public transport was one of the earliest LFIG studies, 'Convincing the Commuter There's a Workable Alternative' [Transport in Zurich], April 1991. The same traffic engineering principles can equally well be applied to inter-urban roads.

253 The various schools are lucidly explained in Lester Thurow, 'Dangerous Currents: The State of Economics', Vintage Books, New York, 1984.

254 Steve Keen, 'Debunking Economics: The Naked Emperor of the Social Sciences', Zed Books, London and New York, 2001.

255 Keen, ibid., page 4.

256 Take such a fascinating and scholarly volume as (ed) John Eatwell, Murray Milgate and Peter Newman, 'The Invisible Hand', The New Palgrave, Macmillan, London and Basingstoke. The authors are almost certainly the world's leading specialists on this subject, but the discourse is entirely historical, biographical and philosophical.

257 Alfred S. Eichner, Introduction to 'Why Economics is not yet a Science', Macmillan, London and Basingstoke, 1983.

258 Homa Katouzian, 'Ideology and Method in Economics', Macmillan, London and Basingstoke, 1980. The present writer has learned a tremendous amount from Katouzian over the years.

259 Katouzian, ibid., Chapter 5, 'Big Science versus Great Science ...' provides an illuminating sociological analysis of the academic profession.

260 Leontiev, Wassily, Foreword to Eichner, op. cit. This was first published in 'Science', the journal of the American Association for the Advancement of Science, Vol. 217, July 1982, pp. 104-5.

261 Eichner, op. cit., page viii.

262 R. G. Lipsey, and K. Lancaster, 'The General Theory of Second Best', reprinted in (ed) M. J. Farrell, 'Readings in Welfare Economics', papers from the Review of Economic Studies, Macmillan, London and Basingstoke, 1973.

263 Alfred E. Kahn, 'The Tyranny of Small Decisions, Market Failures, Imperfections and the Limits of Economics', Kyklos (1966), pp. 23-46.

264 Frederick C. Thayer, F C, analyses this brilliantly in his 'An End to Hierarchy! An End to Competition!', op. cit. 1973, pp. 131-3.

265 Lester G. Telser, 'A Theory of Efficient Co-operation and Competition', Cambridge University Press, New York, 1987; and 'Economic Theory and the Core', University of Chicago Press, 1978.

266 The merits of Telser's analysis persuaded the American Bar Association to stage a 'hypothetical case' on whether electric power producers should be allowed to undertake joint ventures. The conclusions: decisions should rely on the 'rule of reason and not treat the question as a *per se* violation.' In other words, co-operation should not be ruled out on a priori grounds. See Ray Bolze, 'Overview of Key Antitrust issues, Predatory and Strategic Behaviour' in Power Struggle: Antitrust and the Changing Rules of Electric Utility Competition, Americana Bar Association, Chicago, 1996. A lucid summary of the discussion of Telser's arguments is in E. P. Coyle, 'Price Discrimination, Electronic Redlining and Price Fixing in Deregulated Electric Power', American Public Power Association, January 2000.

267 Frank Hahn, 'Reflections on the Invisible Hand' in Lloyds Bank Review, April 1982, no. 144.

268 Hahn, ibid. page 21, where he concludes that 'The age of prophets and of witches is upon us and such an age is not friendly to reason.'

269 It is very difficult to find any precise definitions in the literature. It isn't enough to point to the number of computers or other high-tech devices in an economy or speculate about their effects. To deserve its title, the 'New Economy' must be shown to behave *over the long term* in a qualitatively different way to its predecessors.

270 These themes are developed in Edward Balls, 'Open Macroeconomics in an Open Economy: Labour's Economic Approach – Stability, Growth, Opportunity', LSE Centre for Economic Performance, Occasional Paper No. 13, November 1997. Mr. Balls is economic adviser to Gordon Brown and has no doubt contributed to 'New' Labour's view that monetarism should be supplemented by 'Post Neo-Classical Endogenous Growth Theory'. The latter is an attempt to bring academic economic theory more into line with reality, but it suffers from the kind of defects we discussed earlier. An excellent critique is in Robert Kuttner, 'Everything For Sale: the Virtues and Limits of Markets', op. cit., Chapter 6, 'Markets, Innovation and Growth.'

271 See David Hackett Fischer, 'The Great Wave: Price Revolutions and the Rhythm of History', Oxford University Press, New York, 1996; and Robert Brenner, 'The Boom and the Bubble: the US in the World Economy', Verso, London and New York, 2002.

127

272 Victor Zarnowitz, 'Has the Business Cycle Been Abolished?', Business Economics, October 1998, based on a paper given to the Panel of Economic Advisers to the Congressional Budget Office of the US Congress. Also highly relevant is Bill Martin, 'The New Old Economy', Policy Note 2001, The Levy Economic Institute. Levy is one of the best sources of realistic macro analysis today: www.levy.org

273 Charles Leadbeater, 'Living on Thin Air: the New Economy', Penguin Books, London, 1999. In his Acknowledgements, Leadbeater says that Peter Mandelson, the Secretary of State for Trade and Industry, invited him to develop a White Paper, entitled 'building the Knowledge Driven Economy'. See Patricia Hewitt on this, below.

274 Ibid., page 9.

275 Ibid., Chapter 18. We see here that Leadbeater has provided Blair with material for a thousand articles and speeches.

276 Ibid., pp. xi-xii. The odd thing is that Leadbeater observes many aspects of modern reality, such as increasing concentration of power, massive US public help for advanced industries and the growing insecurity for many people. But he appears to place little weight on such factors. Chapter 17, 'The Power of Fantasy', even begins by saying 'The New Economy seems to offer most people rather little.'

277 Robert J. Gordon, 'Does the "New Economy" Measure Up to the Great Inventions of the Past?', Journal of Economic Perspectives, Vol. 14, no. 4, Fall 2000, pp. 49-74; and the Editors, 'The New Economy: Myth and Reality', Monthly Review, April 2001, Vol. 53, no. 11.

278 On the contrary, as Richard B. Du Boff and Edward S. Herman have shown, concentration is proceeding apace. See their 'Mergers, Concentration and the Erosion of Democracy', Monthly Review, April and May 2001, Vol. 52, No. 11 and Vol. 53, no. 1.

279 Guardian Unlimited, 'Hewitt admits Labour's industry errors', David Gow and Patrick Wintour, 16 May, 2002 http://politics.guardian.co.uk

280 A typical example is Blair's speech to the Party of European Socialists' Congress, Milan, 3 March 1999.

281 Robert M. Solow 'What is Labour Market Flexibility? What is it Good for?', Proceedings of the British Academy, Volume 97, 1998.

282 A typical headline is 'UK caves in on work directive: Rules on management consultation to be phased in after Britain isolated in Luxembourg', Guardian, June 12, 2001.

283 This is based on the writer's frequent dealings with, and visits to, PeoplExpress.

284 Professors A. C. Pigou and Edwin Cannan, quoted by Guy Routh in his 'Unemployment: Economic Perspectives', Macmillan, Basingstoke and London, 1986, page 57.

285 Routh ibid. J. M Keynes, analysed such views in his 'The General Theory of Employment, Interest and Money', Macmillan, London 1954, Chapter 19, 'Changes In Money Wages' with an Appendix on Professor Pigou's 'Theory of Unemployment'.

286 Frank Hahn and Robert Solow, 'A Critical Essay on Modern Macroeconomic Theory', The MIT Press, Cambridge, MA, August 1997.

287 'OECD's View on Employment Protection Legislation', News release, Paris, 13 July 1999. This refers to OECD Employment Outlook for June 1999.

288 Robert M. Solow, op. cit. page 5.

289 The point is not that French and German jobs performance is superior to that of America and Britain. It is that their unemployment cannot be explained by allegedly increasing labour market 'rigidity' because, on the best measure of such 'rigidity', they have had less of it!

290 J. Schmitt and J. Wadsworth, 'Is the OECD Jobs Strategy Behind US and British Employment and Unemployment Success in the 1990s?', Center for Economic Policy Analysis, New School University, New York, April 2002.

291 Bruce Western and Kieran Healy have analysed long term trends in hourly real manufacturing wages for OECD countries in 'Explaining the OECD Wage Slowdown: Recession or Labour Decline?', Princeton University, March 1998. There is a striking downward tendency over a quarter of a century which the authors attribute to the declining power of labour movements. I am indebted to Professor Western for this source.

292 Dean Baker and John Schmitt, 'The Macroeconomic Roots of High European Unemployment: The Impact of Foreign Growth', conference paper on 'Creating Competitive Capacity: Reassessing the Role of US and German Labour Market Institutions in the New Economy', EPI, Washington, October 1998.

293 Gordon Brown, 'Creating Jobs in a Global Economy' in (ed) Lawrence Mishel and John Schmitt, 'Beware the U.S. Model: Jobs and Wages in a Deregulated Economy', Economic Policy Institute, Washington 1995.

294 Employment Policy Foundation, 'Large firms play a dominant role in gross job creation, at least for US manufacturing', The American Workplace 1996, www.epf.org. Steven Davis, John Haltiwanger and Schott Such, 'Small Business and Job Creation: Dissecting the Myth and Reassessing the Facts', quoted in Capital Ideas, Vol. 1, No. 1, Fall 1997, www.uchicago.edu. The latter makes the interesting point that smaller plants show substantially higher *gross* rates of job creation, but not higher *net* rates of creation.

295 J. Rogers Hollingsworth, 'The Institutional Embeddedness of American Capitalism', in C. Crouch and W. Streeck, (eds.) 'Political Economy of Modern Capitalism', Sage, London, 1997.

296 John Schmitt, 'The Wrong Lesson From America', The Guardian, 30 August 1999. This article is also available on the Economic policy Institute web site http://epinet.org/webfeatures/viewpoints.

297 Ibid., page 2. This is Dr Schmitt's overall conclusion.

298 ATW-On-line, Friday 12 April, 2002.

299 Operating managers were enthusiastic while marketing people and top management resisted the idea. The concept was supported by a leading consultant, a large British city authority and Scandinavian travel interests. Nearly every element has, much later, been taken up by the 'new' low fare operators.

300 The mystifying proliferation of fares, and deliberate concealment of their true availability, are leading to court battles and complaints to the Advertising Standards Authority. The new low fare operators are in the forefront of this. Again we see a mish mash of regulatory actions by different bodies.

301 Mick McLean and Tom Rowland, 'The Inmos Saga: A Triumph of National Enterprise?', Frances Pinter, London, 1985. Inmos was a way of securing a British presence in high volume micro-economic components production. The Transputer was a revolutionary 'parallel processing' micro chip.

302 Alfred D. Chandler Jr, 'The Visible Hand: The Managerial Revolution in American Business', Harvard University Press, Cambridge, Mass. and London, 1977; 'Strategy and Structure', MIT Press, Cambridge, Mass. and London, 1969; and 'Scale and Scope: The Dynamics of Industrial Capitalism', Harvard University Press, Cambridge, Mass. and London, 1990.

303 W. Lazonick, 'Business Organisation and the Myth of the Market Economy', Cambridge University Press, 1993.

304 Lazonick. Ibid., Chapter 8, 'Business organisation and economic theory' dismisses the free market economists' attempts to account for these developments in terms of 'transactions costs'.

305 M. Morishima, 'Why Has Japan Succeeded?', Cambridge University Press, 1982. A mathematical economist looks elsewhere to explain Japan's success. Just one of many excellent books on this subject.

306 Ronald Dore, 'Flexible Rigidities: Industrial Policy and Structural Adjustment in the Japanese Economy, 1970-80', Athlone Press, London, 1986; Ronald Dore, 'Taking Japan Seriously, A Confucian Perspective on Leading Economic Issues', Athlone 1987.

307 See Robert Brenner, 'The Economics of Global Turbulence', New Left Review, 229, May/June 1998, pp. 213-226. Of course, there is more to Japanese policy than discussed here, but Brenner is surely right in identifying world industrial over capacity as the source of the problem.

308 All this information is available from the Boeing web sight www.boeing.com

309 There are countless sources here and for the truism that 'this government is unashamedly pro business'. For example, Patricia Hewitt at the Guardian/Observer conference, London, 9 July 2001.

310 M. Mitchell Waldrop, 'Origins of Personal Computing', Scientific American, op. cit. Waldrop's sub title is 'Forget Gates, Jobs and Wozniack.' Much credit goes to the little-recognised J.C.R. Licklider who organised government support in these path breaking areas

311 According to Waldrop, ibid., page 79, Douglas C. Engelbart invented the mouse, on-screen windows, hypertext, full-screen word processing, and many other innovations with lavish funding from the Pentagon, US Air Force and NASA.

312 Erik Arnold and Ken Guy, 'Parallel Convergence: National Strategies in Information Technology', Frances Pinter, London, 1986.

313 US Academy of Sciences, 'Funding a Revolution: Government Support for Computing Research', National Academy Press, Washington 1999.

314 Ibid., page 5 where other examples are given.

315 Eileen Appelbaum, Thomas Bailey, Peter Berg and Arne L. Kalleberg, 'Manufacturing Advantage: Why High-Performance Work Systems Pay Off', Economic Policy Institute, Washington, February 200; and Eileen Appelbaum and Rosemary Batt, 'The New American Workplace: Transforming Work Systems in the United States', ILR Press, Ithaca, NY, 1994.

316 Wallace Roberts, 'The Dimming Down: So Far Electricity Utility Deregulation Has Brought Us Power Shortages and Exorbitant Price Hikes' in The American Prospect, September 25-October 9, 2000. Publicly owned electricity in California – more than 20 per cent of total capacity – has been unaffected by the chaos!

317 The LFIG Transport Group worked out a full strategy for the organic reintegration of the UK railways, written by Don Box, Ross Furby and Peter Reed. This is in the Report of the House of Commons Environment, Transport and Regional Affairs, Transport Sub-Committee, 'The Proposed Strategic Railway Authority and Railway Regulation', HC 286-1.

318 In 1999, a senior transport figure in central Europe complained to us that a British Council symposium had given a highly misleading account of British rail privatisation. Blair's officials are constantly pushing this nonsense in Brussels.

319 This is based on our brief, 'City Perceptions On Rail Privatisation', January 1996, written for Labour shadow spokespersons, with the help of LFIG City experts and communication professionals. The language is authentic 'New' Labour.

320 Civil Aviation Authority, 'Statement of policies on air transport licensing', CAP 501, London, January 1985, para 3.

321 Ibid., paras 3 and 5.

322 CAA, Economic Regulation Group web site www.caa.co/erg

323 This is a major conclusion of S. F. Wheatcroft in his outstanding 'Economics of European Air Transport', Manchester University Press, 1956.

324 Thayer, F.C. 'Rebuilding America: the Case for Economic Regulation', Praeger, New York, 1984. This book is a tonic for anyone who thinks that only Market Theologians write on economics in the USA!

325 Thayer, F. C., 'An End to Hierarchy! An End to Competition', Franklin Watts, New York, 1973, pp. 132-3. Another very thought provoking book!

326 Elliott D. Sclar, 'You Don't Always Get What You Pay For: The Economics of Privatisation.', Century Foundation, Cornell University Press, Ithaca and London, 2000. Professor Sclar's work is a classic source on the experience of privatisation in the USA

327 Ian Mackintosh, 'Sunrise Europe: The Dynamics of Information Technology', Oxford University Press, 1986.

328 The Guardian, 'Blair faces fight on TV controls' and 'TV drama in the making', 29 July 2002.

329 According to Dr John Reid, the party would not sit in judgement on 'those who wish to contribute to the Labour Party', reported in 'Labour's Farewell to Morals', Tribune 17 May 2002.

330 Beth Marie Kosir, 'Modesty to Majesty: the Development of the Codpiece', Richard III Society, American Branch, www.r3.org

331 A striking illustration is the 'seven strong strategy board to oversee the work of the department and provide central direction to the DTI's overall strategy', announced on 22 November 2001. According to Patricia Hewitt, this will ensure that DTI is 'truly focussed on its customers' needs'. The TUC apparently learned of this development via the press. See www.eiro.eurofound.i.e./2001/12/Feature/UK0112132F Equally bizarre is the handing over to private lending institutions of the power to control many safety critical decisions on the London Underground. See Transport for London , PPP News, 21 June 2002.

332 Robert Worcester and Roger Mortimore, 'Explaining Labour's Landslide', Politico's, London 1999, give the lion's share of the credit for Labour's victory to the Conservatives.

The Author

At the 1994 launch of Labour's first Public and Private Finance initiative, John Prescott paid a public tribute to Peter Reed who chaired the Transport Study Group of the Labour Finance and Industry Group from 1991 to 2000. In that capacity, working with some of the country's leading finance and transport specialists, Peter helped John Prescott to develop Labour's flagship 'modernisation' policy. In those ten years, he also gave professional advice to no less than six Labour shadow transport ministers.

Peter's professional career began at London Transport where he gained commercial and operational experience in urban buses, road haulage, underground and main-line railways, and held posts in Planning and Finance. Later he became an Economic Adviser at the Ministry of Transport, responsible for inter-urban modelling, and advice on railway and road-haulage policy, including work on the 1968 Transport Act. As an academic economist at the University of Reading, where the Ministry of Transport funded his research unit, he continued as a part time adviser to the Ministry and the Department of Environment. During this period, he published a text-book on the *Economics of Public Enterprise*.

Peter Reed joined the Civil Aviation Authority soon after its formation as Head of Economics. He was subsequently promoted to Head of Economic Policy and Licensing, and then again to General Manager Economic Regulation. In the latter role, Peter was responsible for all economic regulation of British aviation and for advice to Government on matters like airport planning. On the international front, amongst other activities, Peter was head of the UK economics team in the Bermuda II negotiations and leader of the British delegation to the ECAC/Eurpol group which initiated the process of European air services liberalisation.

After leaving the CAA, Peter advised major airlines in Australia, Britain and USA, and has served as a member of the International Air Transport Association's group of world regulatory experts. In his capacity as Economic Adviser to the British Air Line Pilots'

Association, he led the process of establishing the first multinational trade union, the European Cockpit Association. Over many years, he has also advised the Aviation Forum, the collective body of the UK trade unions with members in air transport.

The son of a Yorkshire miner, Peter Reed joined the Labour Party more than half a century ago.

Common Ownership
Clause IV and the Labour Party
by Ken Coates

Opposition to Tony Blair's decision to emasculate the Labour Party's constitution by eradicating Clause IV on common ownership was strongest in the European Parliamentary Labour Party. This book traces the arguments, and shows the continuing relevance of socialism, whatever the evolution of the Labour Party and however many MEPs it purges.

'Socialism certainly needs to be re-invented. Old-fashioned nationalisation will not be restored, any more than the monasteries, the patrimony of the poor in the middle ages. But common ownership is more and more the necessary response to runaway private acquisitiveness, and the infinite destruction wrought by greed.'

ISBN 0 85124 573 0 hardback   108 pages   £25.00
ISBN 0 85124 574 9 paperback   £5.99

also

Labour and the Commonweal
Tony Blair, Ken Coates, William Morris, Sydney Webb, John Hughes et al   20 pages   £1

Available post-free from
SPOKESMAN BOOKS
Russell House, Bulwell Lane, Nottingham, NG6 0BT
Tel. 0115 9708318 Fax 0115 9420433
e-mail: elfeuro@compuserve.com

Please send cheque with order, payable to 'Bertrand Russell House'.
Publications list, including Socialist Renewal titles, available on request and at
www.spokesmanbooks.com